W0189328

English for Telephoning

David Gordon Smith

SHORT COURSE
SERIES

Autor	David Gordon Smith, Berlin
kritische Durchsicht	Marion Grussendorf, Köln Louise Kennedy, Schenefeld
Verlagsredaktion	Janan Barksdale
Redaktionelle Mitarbeit	Katja Hartmann, Christine House, Fritz Preuss (Wortliste), Rebecca Syme
Bildredaktion	Uta Hübner
Gesamtgestaltung und technische Umsetzung	Sylvia Lang
Bildquellen	*Titel:* Getty Images *Cartoons und Illustrationen:* Oxford Designers & Illustrators *Fotos:* BananaStock: S. 6, 10, 14, 19, 20, 21, 26, 28, 35, 38, 42, 45; COMSTOCK: S. 25, 45 (3); Corbis GmbH: S. 30, 31, 33/Mark M Lawrence; C. Gebhard: S. 7; Getty Images: S. 5, 12, 19, 26, 34, 40

Nicht alle Copyright-Inhaber konnten ermittelt werden; deren Urheberrechte werden hiermit vorsorglich und ausdrücklich anerkannt.

www.cornelsen.de

Die Links zu externen Webseiten Dritter, die in diesem Lehrwerk angegeben sind, wurden vor Drucklegung sorgfältig auf ihre Aktualität geprüft. Der Verlag übernimmt keine Gewähr für die Aktualität und den Inhalt dieser Seiten oder solcher, die mit ihnen verlinkt sind.

1. Auflage, 4. Druck 2011/06

Alle Drucke dieser Auflage sind inhaltlich unverändert und können im Unterricht nebeneinander verwendet werden.

© 2004 Cornelsen Verlag, Berlin

Das Werk und seine Teile sind urheberrechtlich geschützt. Jede Nutzung in anderen als den gesetzlich zugelassenen Fällen bedarf der vorherigen schriftlichen Einwilligung des Verlages. Hinweis zu den §§ 46, 52 a UrhG: Weder das Werk noch seine Teile dürfen ohne eine solche Einwilligung eingescannt und in ein Netzwerk eingestellt oder sonst öffentlich zugänglich gemacht werden. Dies gilt auch für Intranets von Schulen und sonstigen Bildungseinrichtungen.

Druck: CS-Druck CornelsenStürtz, Berlin

ISBN 978-3-464-01873-6

 Inhalt gedruckt auf säurefreiem Papier aus nachhaltiger Forstwirtschaft.

Inhalt

Vorwort

Es gibt inzwischen kaum einen Beruf, bei dem Telefonieren nicht zum Arbeitsalltag gehört – und im Zuge der Globalisierung werden geschäftliche Telefonate auch zunehmend auf Englisch geführt. Aber selbst für Arbeitnehmer mit guten Sprachkenntnissen stellen englische Telefonate oft eine schwierige Hürde dar. Selten ist man auf englischsprachige Anrufe vorbereitet, zudem können mangelnde Klangqualität sowie die nicht sichtbare Mimik und Gestik des Gesprächspartners eine reibungslose Kommunikation erschweren.

Doch zum Glück gibt es spezifische sprachliche Charakteristika deren Kenntnis es Ihnen ermöglicht, englische Telefonate gewandt und kompetent zu meistern: standardisierte Gesprächsabläufe, situationstypische Redewendungen sowie Konversationsstrategien, mit denen Sie sich auch in schwierigen Telefongesprächen behaupten können.

English for Telephoning bietet Ihnen Training in allen genannten Bereichen und hilft Ihnen somit, Ihre englischen Telefonate erfolgreich und selbstbewusst zu führen.

English for Telephoning besteht aus sechs Units, denen jeweils eine bestimmte, für das Gespräch am Telefon nützliche Fertigkeit zugrunde liegt. Basiskenntnisse werden dabei vorrangig zu Beginn, fortgeschrittene Kenntnisse eher gegen Ende des Buchs vermittelt. Dennoch ist die Einhaltung der Unit-Reihenfolge nicht verbindlich, bei Bedarf können auch nur besonders relevante oder interessante Units ausgewählt werden.

Am Anfang jeder Unit steht das sogenannte **Picking up**, das aus einer kurzen Übung, einem Quiz oder einem Fragebogen besteht. Besonders der Fragebogen ermöglicht Ihnen, Ihr eigenes Telefonverhalten zu verstehen und ggf. zu hinterfragen. Realistische Hörtexte (in Form von Telefondialogen auf der beiliegenden **Audio-CD**) dienen dem Training von Hörverständnis sowie der Demonstration nützlicher Höflichkeits- und Kommunikationsstrategien und der Einführung wichtiger Redemittel und Vokabeln. Eine Vielzahl unterschiedlicher Übungen bietet Ihnen die Möglichkeit, Ihr Wissen zu überprüfen, neue Redewendung zu lernen oder grammatische Kernstrukturen zu üben. Infokästchen weisen auf sprachliche Besonderheiten hin. Im Rahmen von Rollenspielen (passende Rollenbeschreibungen in den **Partner files**) wenden Sie die erworbenen sprachlichen Kenntnisse und Fähigkeiten in offeneren Gesprächssituationen an. Am Unit-Ende befindet sich jeweils ein Abschnitt namens **Hanging up**, bestehend aus einem thematisch passenden (fakultativen) Lesetext, der zu interessanten Diskussionen anregt. Mittels eines Kreuzworträtsels können Sie in **Test yourself!** noch einmal spielerisch prüfen, was Sie in den zurückliegenden sechs Units gelernt haben.

Im Anhang von **English for Telephoning** finden Sie den **Answer key**, mit dem Sie Ihre Antworten selbstständig überprüfen können. Der Anhang enthält außerdem die **Partner files** sowie eine **A–Z word list**. Mit Hilfe der Zusammenstellung der **Useful phrases and vocabulary** können Sie auch am Arbeitsplatz die häufigsten Redewendungen und Begriffe, die Sie für ein englischsprachiges Telefonat benötigen, schnell und einfach nachschlagen.

1 "Shall I put you through?"

PICKING UP

Work with a partner. Ask him or her the questions below and make a note of the answers. Then tell the class what you found out.

CAN I CALL YOU BACK LATER WHEN I'VE FINISHED "ENGLISH FOR TELEPHONING?"

1 How often do you make phone calls in English?

2 When was the last time you made or received a phone call in English? How was it?

3 Who do you normally speak English to on the phone? Are they native speakers or non-native speakers of English?

4 What do you find most difficult about telephoning in English?

5 Describe your worst experience with an English phone call.

2–4

1 **Three people are calling the company Micah Information Systems. Listen to the three dialogues and complete the table.**

	CALL 1	CALL 2	CALL 3
Who is calling?			
Who does he/she want to speak to?			
Does he/she get through? if not, why not?			
What will happen next?			

British English	American English
The line is engaged.	The line is busy.
mobile (phone)	cell (phone)

2 **Listen again and complete the sentences from the dialogues.**

2-4

1 Micah Information Systems. Sylvia _____ .

2 I'll _____ Mr Seide you _____ .

3 It's Karen Miller _____ .

4 I actually _____ to speak to Maria.

5 Just _____ on a moment while I make the

   _____ .

6 I'm _____ Maria's line is _____ .

7 I'll try _____ later.

8 Let me just _____ a pen.

9 Nice to _____ from you.

10 I'm actually talking to someone on the other _____ .

Which sentences (1–10) can be used ...

a to say who you are? _1,_____
b to open a conversation politely? _____
c to say who you want to speak to? _____
d to put a caller through to another person? _____

e to say that somebody (or you) can't talk now? _____
f to say you will call again later? _____
g to take or leave a message? _____

3 **Match the halves to make questions from the dialogues.**

1 Could I speak	my mobile number?
2 Can I take	through to her?
3 Could you ask	have your number?
4 Could you tell me	back in ten minutes?
5 Does Mr Seide	your name again?
6 Is she there	a message?
7 Shall I put you	ask what it's about?
8 Can I just	at the moment?
9 Can I call you	to Jörg Seide, please?
10 Have you got	him to call me back?

Now match these answers to the questions. Sometimes more than one answer is possible.

a Certainly.
b Yes, he does.
c Sure, no problem.
d My name is John Ellis.
e Yes, I have.
f That would be great.

g Yes, she is.
h I'm afraid he's in a meeting.
i I need to ask her about the project meeting next week.
j Yes, please.

4 We can normally say the same thing in a more formal or less formal way.
Find pairs of expressions with the same meaning and complete the table.

~~Can I speak to Bob, please?~~   Certainly.   ~~Could I speak to Bob, please?~~

Thanks.   What's it about?   Could you please hold?   Hang on a moment.

Can I just ask what it's about?   Shall I put you through to her?   Sure.

Do you want to speak to her?   Thank you.

MORE FORMAL	LESS FORMALL
Could I speak to Bob, please?	*Can I speak to Bob, please?*

5 There are different ways to give our names on the telephone. Match the sentences to the explanations. (Careful: one sentence below is not used on the telephone!)

1   This is Gordon Wallis.
2   It's Gordon (Wallis) here.
3   Here is Gordon Wallis.
4   Gordon (Wallis) speaking.

a   You say this when you answer the phone.
b   You say this when you call a company and you don't know the person who answers the phone.
c   You say this when you call someone you know.

USING FIRST NAMES

Whether we use first names or family names with people in English normally depends on the relationship we have with them. Here are some tips.

- As a general rule, do what the other person does. So if the other person uses your first name, use their first name when you speak to them. One important exception: if the other person has a much higher status than you (for example if you are a secretary and they are a manager) then sometimes it's better to use their family name, even if they use your first name. It depends on the company culture.

- If it's the very first time you speak to a person, you should probably use their family name.
- If you've had contact with the person before (even if it was only on the phone), you can normally use first names.
- If the person is an important business contact, you should definitely try to use first names, if appropriate. It's a sign of a close working relationship.

6 Look at – or listen to – the three phone calls in Exercise 1 again. Who uses first names, and who uses family names? Why?

2–4

GIVING 'BAD' NEWS

It's very common for native speakers to use 'I'm afraid' or 'I'm sorry' when giving 'bad' news, for example when saying someone isn't available.

I'm afraid Mr Seide is in a meeting.
I'm sorry, but Mr Seide is in a meeting.

If you don't use 'I'm afraid' or 'I'm sorry', the sentence sounds very direct and impolite to a native speaker.

The word **'actually'** is also often used to make a statement more polite. For example, it can be used:
- instead of saying the word 'no': *"Does he have your phone number?" "**Actually**, I don't think he does."*
- when we change the subject (eg when we change from small talk to talking business): *"I can imagine. Listen, Sylvia, I **actually** wanted to speak to Maria."*
- to say something which is inconvenient or annoying for the other person, in a polite way: *"Can I call you back? I'm **actually** talking to someone on the other line."*

Remember that 'actually' is **not** the same as the German *aktuell*, which is normally translated as 'current(ly)'.

7 **Rewrite the underlined sentences below with *I'm afraid or actually*.**

1 <u>I'm trying to get through to Jake Woodward</u>. He asked me to call him this morning.
   I'm actually trying to get through …
2 Helga Brecht. You're from Germany, aren't you? – <u>No, I'm from Austria.</u>
3 Can I talk to Kevin Shields? – <u>He's not here</u>.
4 Would you like to leave a message? – <u>No, I'll call back later</u>.
5 Can I call you tomorrow? – <u>I won't be in the office tomorrow</u>.
6 <u>Heather's line is engaged</u>. Shall I tell her to call you back?

8 **Make excuses for why your boss doesn't want to come to the phone. Try to use *I'm afraid*, *I'm sorry* or *actually* in each sentence. Remember that you don't always need to tell the truth when making an excuse!**

EXAMPLE

I'm afraid she's unavailable. She's actually in a meeting at the moment.

REDEWENDUNG

unavailable at the moment
out of the office today/this afternoon
on a business trip
in a meeting
on another line

9 **Work with a partner to practise the dialogue below.**

A		B
Answer phone.	→	Say hello and make some small talk.
Respond.	←	Change subject and ask to speak to somebody.
Person is unavailable. Say why and offer to take message.	← →	
		Leave message.
Take message.	← →	Say thank you and goodbye.

10 **Often when we telephone we have to deal with communication problems. Listen to the dialogues and match the problem to the call. (Sometimes more than one answer is possible.)**

CALL

a The caller is speaking too quietly. . . . . ☐

b The person called didn't understand what the caller said. 7

c The person called wants the caller to say something again. . . . . ☐

d The caller is speaking too fast. . . . . ☐

e The caller has called someone by mistake. . . . . ☐

f The person called doesn't know how to write a word. . . . . ☐

g The phone itself is making a lot of noise. . . . . ☐

h The previous call was cut off and the caller has to call the other person back. . . . . ☐

Now complete the phrases from the dialogues with words from the list. Then listen again to check your answers.

slowly • up • cut • line • catch • spell • could • wrong

1 Sorry, I didn't _____ that.

2 Sorry, _____ you repeat that, please?

3 Sorry, can you speak _____ a bit, please?

4 Sorry, I think you have the _____ number.

5 Sorry, this is a really bad _____ .

6 Sorry, we got _____ off.

7 Sorry, could you _____ that for me, please?

8 Sorry, could you say that a bit more _____ , please?

11 **Work with a partner to make two phone calls. Look at the useful phrases below before you read your role card in the partner files.**

PARTNER FILES ➤ File 01, p. 48
File 01, p. 50

USEFUL PHRASES

Giving your name
Gail Jones speaking.
This is Robert Smith from ABC Enterprises.
Hello, Jane. It's Barbara Schütz here.

Getting through to the right person
Could/Can I speak to Mark, please?
I'd like to speak to Ellen Baker, please.
I actually wanted to speak to Pat.
Is Pascal there at the moment?

Making the connection
Shall I put you through to him/her?
Can I just ask what it's about
Could you please hold?
Just hang on a moment while I make the connection.

When the person isn't available
I'm afraid his/her line is engaged.
I'm afraid Pat isn't available at the moment.
I'm afraid she is in a meeting.
Can I take a message?
Would you like to call back later?

12 **Complete the crossword, then rearrange the letters in the orange squares to find the mystery word.**

The mystery word is ☐ ☐ ☐ ☐ ☐ ☐ ☐ ☐ ☐

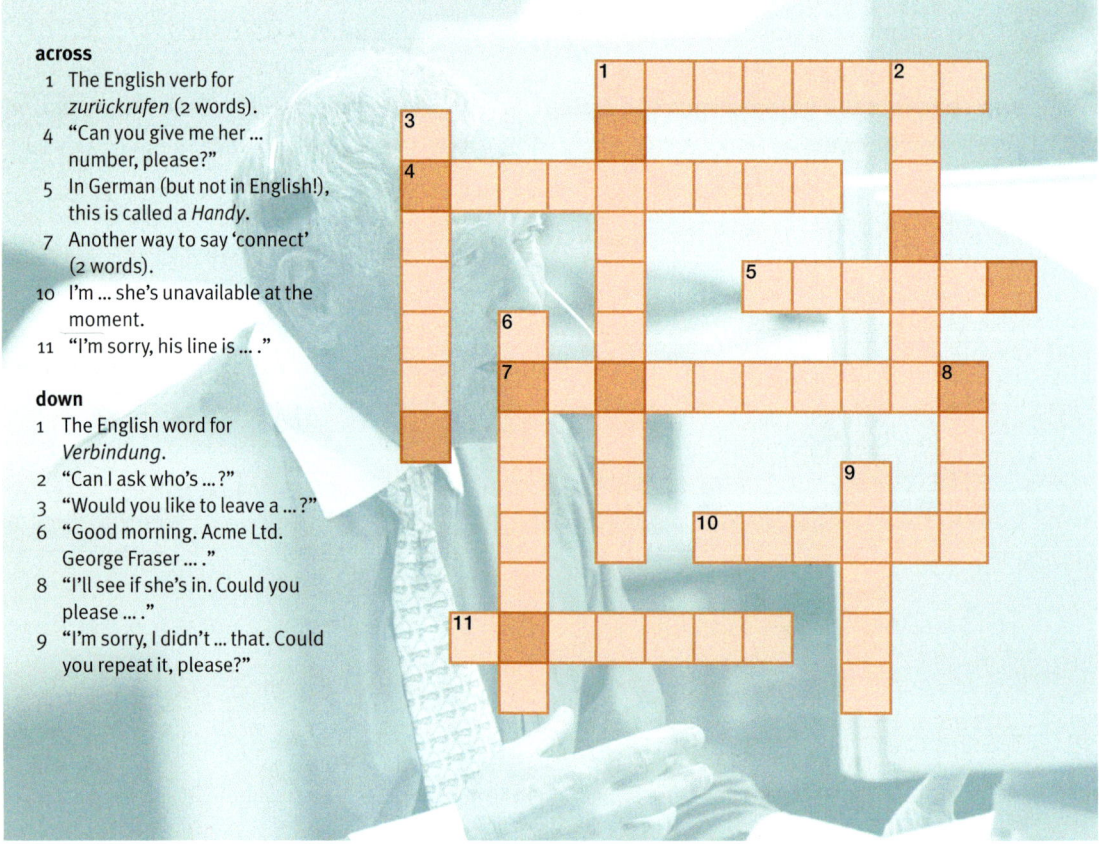

across
1 The English verb for *zurückrufen* (2 words).
4 "Can you give me her ... number, please?"
5 In German (but not in English!), this is called a *Handy*.
7 Another way to say 'connect' (2 words).
10 I'm ... she's unavailable at the moment.
11 "I'm sorry, his line is ... ."

down
1 The English word for *Verbindung*.
2 "Can I ask who's ...?"
3 "Would you like to leave a ...?"
6 "Good morning. Acme Ltd. George Fraser ... ."
8 "I'll see if she's in. Could you please ... ."
9 "I'm sorry, I didn't ... that. Could you repeat it, please?"

13 **Translate these sentences. Try to use expressions from this unit.**

1 Elke Heide am Apparat.

2 Hier ist Jan Müller. Kann ich bitte Frau Sanders sprechen?

3 Ich rufe später zurück.

4 Brenda ist heute unterwegs.

5 Haben Sie meine Handy-Nummer?

6 Herr Schmidt ist heute leider nicht im Haus.

7 Ich sage ihm, dass Sie angerufen haben.

ANGING UP

What advice would you give to someone to help them telephone successfully? Work with a partner to make a list of tips. Then read the article and discuss the questions.

Successful telephoning

Phone calls can often be challenging in your own language, but when you're speaking a foreign language they are even more difficult. There's no body language to help you, the audio quality is not always perfect and there is more time pressure than in a face-to-face conversation. Below are some tips to make telephoning in English less stressful.

1 If you have to make a difficult phone call, spend a few minutes preparing first. Think about what you want from the phone call. What might the other person say? Make notes of English phrases you can use during the call.

2 Try to relax. Make sure you have enough time for the call, and don't hurry. It's better to have a successful ten-minute call than an unsuccessful five-minute call.

3 Sometimes receiving an unexpected call can be very stressful. To give yourself some time to prepare for the call, you might want to tell a 'white lie' (*"I'm sorry, I'm actually in a meeting right now. Can I call you back in ten minutes?"*) and call back when you feel more confident.

4 It's important to make a little small talk with the other person before you talk business, but don't spend too long chatting. Get to the point of the call quickly. If you're talking to a native English speaker, listen for words like 'well', 'so' and 'anyway' — these are signals that it's time to talk business.

5 Speak more slowly and at a lower pitch than you would during a face-to-face conversation. It makes you sound confident, helps the other person to understand you, and calms you down if you are nervous.

6 Don't be afraid to ask a caller to repeat something (*"I'm sorry, I still didn't catch that. Could you say it again more slowly?"*). It's better for the caller to repeat a piece of information five times than for you to write down the wrong information.

7 Smile! Although it sounds strange, the other person can hear if you are smiling – it makes your voice sound friendlier.

OVER TO YOU

What is the thing you find most difficult on the telephone? How could you make it easier?

Can you think of five things you could do to improve your telephoning skills in English (eg record English calls and listen to them with your English teacher, or telephone an English-speaking friend for practice)?

2 "Could you spell that for me?"

PICKING UP

How good are you at giving information over the phone? Do this quiz on numbers and symbols. Compare your answers with a partner's, then check your answers in the key.

1 How do you say these numbers in English?

   (a) 647

   (b) 9,235

   (c) 1,574,389

   (d) 1.955

   (e) €15.40

   (f) 0049 30 29706634

I CAN THINK OF AT LEAST 15 REASONS WHY I SHOULD FIRE YOU!

SORRY – DID YOU SAY 15 OR 50?

2 What does a comma (,) show in an English number? And a point (.)?

3 What are these symbols called in English?

   (a) (b) (c)   (d)

bob_jones@abc-company.com

   (e) / _____

   (f) \ _____

   (g) # _____

   (h) * _____

   (i) (_____

   (j)) _____

See page 68 for more information about saying numbers and symbols in English.

13–14

1 Arno Maier works in a small import/export company in Hamburg. Listen to the two calls Arno makes and receives, and correct the mistakes in the notes.

relay switch
model RS 788

unit price:
1000 units + €1.65
2000 units + €11.39

Misha Oberemok
delivery address

Mitscevitch Ulittsa 6
97000 Kiev
Fax no. (+380 44)
244 4240

VOCABULARY ASSISTANT

delivery address *Lieferadresse*
digit *Zahl, Ziffer*
to drop *fallen* to get sent off *abgeschickt werden*
relay switch *Relaisschalter*
unit price *Stückpreis*

2 **Listen to the dialogues again and complete the phrases below.**

−14

Call 1

I have a question _____¹ your relay

switches. Are you the _____² person

to ask?

What _____³ your question?

Could you _____⁴ me what the unit

price would be for orders over a thousand

units?

It was the RS 877 you said, _____⁵?

Sorry, I didn't _____⁶ the second price.

Call 2

I'm _____¹ about the order you faxed

us yesterday.

I just wanted to _____² it.

Do you have a _____³?

Would you like me to _____⁴ that for

you?

Let me just _____⁵ that back to you.

Sorry, what was the post code _____⁶?

HOW TO BE LESS DIRECT

Generally in English, the less direct a sentence is, the more polite it is. For example, we often use
the past tense (*was, wanted*) instead of the present tense (*is, want*). The past tense is more polite,
because it's less direct.

> *What **was** your question?*
> *I just **wanted** to check ...*
> *I **wanted** to ask about ...*

Similarly, we often use 'could' and 'would' to make questions or statements less direct.

> ***Could** you tell me what the price **would be**? (instead of **Can** you tell me what the price **is**?)*
> *What **would be** your preferred means of payment? (instead of What **is** your ...?)*

3 **Rewrite the sentences below to make them less direct.**

1 What is your question? *What was your question?* _____

2 Can you tell me your name? _____

3 I just want to check the address. _____

4 What is your name again? _____

5 What do you want to know? _____

6 What is your charge for delivery? _____

7 How long does it take to send it? _____

8 I want to ask if you have time to meet tomorrow. _____

_____

ACTIVE LISTENING STRATEGIES

Active listening strategies can help you to communicate more effectively on the telephone.

When listening, say words like 'right', 'uh huh', 'got you' or 'yeah' every few seconds to show that you are paying attention. The other person feels more relaxed because it's clear that you are there and actively listening to them.

Check each piece of information that the other person gives you – even if you *think* you have understood everything perfectly, you might have actually *misunderstood* something the other person said. You can do this by ...

- 'Echoing' (repeating what the other perso said, to make sure you understood correctly):
  A *We can deliver on Tuesday.*
  B *Tuesday. Right.*

- Asking for clarification:
  A *Our address is 40 George Street.*
  B *Sorry, did you say 40 or 14?*

- Reading numbers and other important pieces of information back to the other person:
  A *My number is 2389 5354.*
  B *Let me just read that back to you. So that's 2389 5354.*

- You can also ask the other person to read a number back if they don't do it themselves:
  Can you just read that back to me?

4   **Complete these excerpts from a telephone conversation with words from the box.**

> And your name was • Did you say • Let me just read that back to you. • So that's • Sorry, was that • To Germany?

Karin   Well, first of all, how long would it take to ship a consignment to Germany?

George   _____[1]. I would say between a week and ten days by sea. We could also send a shipment via air freight, but that would naturally be more expensive.

Karin   _____[2] a week to ten days?

George   Yes, that's right.

• • • • • • •

Karin   So that's 40 for Hamburg, then 3861 3453.

George   _____[3] 3453 or 2453?

Karin   It's 34 53.

George   Right. _____[4] It's 01149 40 3861 3453.

Karin   Yes, that's right.

• • • • • • •

George   Great. _____[5] Karin ...?

Karin   Lubitz. That's spelt L-U-B-I-T-Z.

George   _____[6] Karin Lubitz.

   L-U-B-I-T-Z. Got you.

5 **Check that you've understood. Ask about the highlighted information. (More than one answer is possible each time.)**

1 I would like to order 50 units. *Sorry, did you say 50 or 15 units? / OK, so that's 50 units.* _____

2 Our address is 98 King Street, Hull. _____

3 My phone number is 091 210 3885. _____

4 The meeting is on Thursday. _____

5 My name is Oliver Prentice. _____

6 The new price is €72.90. _____

6 **Do you know how to say the alphabet in English?**

Complete this table by putting the letters of the alphabet into the correct columns according to how you say them. For example, C [siː] goes into the same column as B [biː], because they have the same vowel sound. If a letter doesn't fit into an existing column, put it into a new column.

1	2	3	4	5	6	7
A	B					
	C					

SPELLING

Although there is an official English spelling alphabet (developed by NATO and used by the military and by radio operators), most English speakers do not know it. Instead, they use common words or personal names to spell words. For example, to spell NATO, an English speaker might say:

That's N for Neil, A for apple, T for Thomas, O for orange.

Notice that in English we say *N **for** Neil* or *N **as in** Neil (AE)*, not ~~N like Neil~~.

7 **Work with a partner to practise spelling. You'll find a list of place names in your file. Spell the names in your list for your partner and write down the names your partner spells for you.**

PARTNER FILES File 02, p. 48 File 02, p. 50

8 **Write the email and website addresses in words.**

1 alan.thompson@hotmail.com *Alan dot Thompson at hotmail dot com*

2 www.gopher-systems.com *w w w* dot gopher hyphen** systems dot com*

3 kevin.stevens@afg-consulting.ca _____

4 margaret_peterson@zebra.it _____

5 www.rent-a-car.com _____

6 (your email address) _____

7 (your company website address) _____

* Remember that the letter 'w' is pronounced 'double
you' in English.

** Some people say 'dash' instead of 'hyphen'. However we don't
normally say 'minus' in email addresses (unlike in German).

Now practise reading the addresses out loud.

9 **Make sentences from this unit. Start at the numbered word, then move one square at a time
(left, right, up or down).**

1 Do	**2** Let	me	just	check	that.	person	to	ask?	**3** I'm
you	have	that	read	just	**4** Are	right	the	about	calling
5 What	a	back	**6** Let	me	you	the	order	you	**7** Would
would	pen?	to	back	to	you?	**8** What	you	like	me
you	like	you.	get	give	me	was	faxed	us	to
know?	to	that	and	just	your	your	question?	yesterday.	spell
9 Can	I	check	**10** Can	you	phone	number?	you?	for	that

**Use the phrases you found above to complete the two dialogues. (Sometimes more than one
answer is possible.)**

Kevin   Mahoney Engineering. Kevin speaking.

Fiona   Hello Kevin. This is Fiona from ALP Supplies. _____ A.

I have a question about one of the items. _____ B.

Kevin   I'm not sure, but I'll do my best! _____ C.

Fiona   Well, the item number HG 892375 is out of stock at the moment, and I wanted to ask if the
HG 892376 would be okay instead. It's almost the same model.

Kevin   Oh Fiona, I'm not totally sure. _____ D.

Fiona	Sure, no problem.
Kevin	Great. _____ ^E.
Fiona	Of course. It's 0248 294 413.
Kevin	Right. _____ ^F. Your number is 0248 294 413.
Fiona	That's right.
Kevin	Okay Fiona, I'll talk to my boss and I'll call you back later today.
Fiona	Great. Bye now.
Kevin	Bye.

• • • • • • •

Kathy	Voland Information Services. Kathy speaking.
Paul	Hi Kathy. It's Paul here. I just have a quick question about the software you installed for us last week.
Kathy	Oh, hi Paul. Nice to hear from you. _____ ^G.
Paul	Well, I'm afraid we've lost the dummy user name for the test set-up. Can you give it to us again?
Kathy	Sure. No problem. _____ ^H.
Paul	Yes, I do. Fire away.
Kathy	OK. The user name is 'Joe.Bloggs'. _____ ^I.
Paul	Yes please.
Kathy	OK. It's J-O-E dot B-L-O-G-G-S.
Paul	_____ ^J. The user name is 'Joe.Bloggs', spelt J-O-E dot B-L-O-G-G-S.
Kathy	That's right.
Paul	Well, thanks very much Kathy.
Kathy	You're welcome. Bye now.

10 **Work with a partner to make two phone calls. Look at the useful phrases below before you look at the information in your file.**

> PARTNER FILES → File 03, p. 48
> File 03, p. 50

USEFUL PHRASES

Opening the call	**Exchanging information**	**Checking information**
I'm calling about …	What was your question?	Would you like me to spell that for you?
I have a question about …	What would you like to know?	Did you say …?
I wanted to ask about …	Could you tell me …?	Sorry, I didn't catch that.
Are you the right person to ask?		Let me just read that back to you.
		Let me just check that.

11 **Translate these sentences. Try to use expressions from this unit.**

1 Haben Sie etwas zum Schreiben?
2 Die Bestellnummer ist Anton-Emil-Viktor-null-zwei-sechs.
3 War das ‚D' wie ‚Dora' oder ‚B' wie ‚Berta'?
4 Seine E-Mail-Adresse lautet ‚Tom minus Baker at Martins Punkt D E'.
5 Entschuldigung, das habe ich nicht ganz verstanden. Haben Sie 13 oder 30 gesagt?

Read the article and discuss the questions.

Get active with your listening

Imagine you are calling an important business contact. The person says he is in a hurry and only has five minutes for the call. While you are talking, you hear him typing on his computer keyboard, and he continually interrupts you while you are trying to talk. How would you feel?

The above description is an example of a bad listener. Everyone learns at school how to read and write, but normally we are never taught how to listen. However, effective listening is one of the most important communication skills.

Here are some things you can do to improve your active listening skills.

1   Remove distractions. Make sure the place where you are telephoning isn't too hot, too cold, too noisy or too uncomfortable.

2   When you're on the phone, don't type, tidy your desk or organize your papers. The noises you make will tell your partner that you're not listening.

3   Forget about your own problems and tasks while talking to your partner. You can't concentrate on what someone else is saying if you are thinking about your 'to do' list.

4   Regularly summarize what your conversation partner has told you, to show that you are listening ("So what you mean is …", "If I understood you correctly, you want to …"). This can also help your partner to move forward in the conversation.

5   Be honest with your partner. If you weren't paying attention to what they said, or if their English is too difficult, tell them and ask them to repeat what they said ("Sorry, could you say that again?", "I'm sorry, but I'm finding you difficult to understand. Could you maybe try to talk in simpler English, please?").

6   Wait until the other person has stopped talking before you decide what to say next. If you are constantly thinking about your response, you won't be able to concentrate on what they are saying. Use phrases like "let me see", "I see what you mean", or "I just need to think for a moment" to give yourself time to think about what to say next.

7   Learn listening skills from other people. Pay attention to how other people (especially native speakers) show you that they are listening.

OVER TO YOU

Are you a good listener? Why do you think that?

How could you improve your own listening skills?

Can you think of people you know who are good/bad listeners? How do you feel when you speak to them?

3 "Let me get back to you on that."

CKING UP

Look at these answering machine and voicemail greetings from four different companies. Which is the best in your opinion? Why?

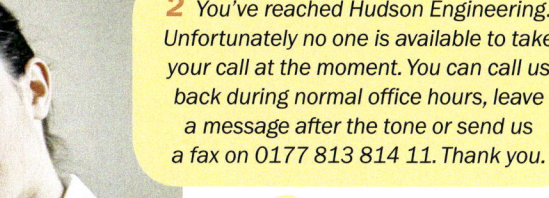

1 Hello. You've reached Yo-Yo Design. Leave a message.

2 You've reached Hudson Engineering. Unfortunately no one is available to take your call at the moment. You can call us back during normal office hours, leave a message after the tone or send us a fax on 0177 813 814 11. Thank you.

3 Hello. Fusion Financial Services, Joel Parker speaking. There's no one here at the moment, but you can leave a message after the beep and we'll call you back as soon as we can.

4 Hi, this is Cecilia's voicemail. I'm out of the office until the 5th. If it's urgent, please contact Jeff Young on extension 439. Thanks.

Does your company or do you have an answering machine or voicemail greeting in English? If so, what is it? If not, work with a partner to write one.

🇬🇧 **British English**	**American English** 🇺🇸
(also) answerphone	answering machine
send us a fax on 897 543	send us a fax at 543-2111
on extension 439	at extension 438

–16

1 Listen and write down the messages.

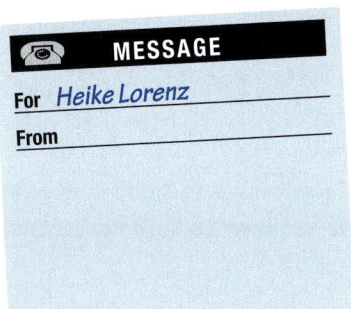

☎ **MESSAGE**

For *Heike Lorenz*

From

☎ **MESSAGE**

For

From

VOCABULARY ASSISTANT V

to confirm *bestätigen*
prospective *potenziell, voraussichtlich*

What is wrong with the second message? What would your reaction be if you received it?

2 Listen to the answering-machine greeting and the first caller's message again and complete the phrases.

You've_____ [1] Leze Logistics. _____ [2] no one is _____ [3] to take your call at the moment. Please _____ [4] a message after the _____ [5].

- _____ [6] is Walter Jackson _____ [7] for Heike Lorenz.
- Maybe you can _____ [8] back to me as soon as you've _____ [9] the date and time with everyone.
- I think you have my number already, but here it is _____ [10], just in _____ [11].
- Hope to speak to you _____ [12].

HOW TO STRUCTURE A MASSAGE

It's important to structure your message clearly when you speak on an answering machine. Here is one way to do it.

- Say who you are and (if necessary) who you are leaving the message for: *Hello, this is … calling for …*
- Explain the message step by step: *I'm calling about … /I just wanted to confirm …*
- Say what action you would like the other person to take (if any): *Maybe you could get back to me … / Could you call me back …?*
- Make sure the other person knows how to contact you: *Here's my number … /You can reach me on …*

Don't forget to keep your message as short as possible and to talk slowly and clearly.

---

3 First call Walter Jackson back (message 1) and speak on his voicemail to confirm the date and time of the meeting. Then use your notes from Exercise 1 to rewrite Seth Prescott's message (message 2).

4 Work with a partner to practise leaving messages.

PARTNER FILES File 04, p. 48
File 04, p. 50

5 **Anke Schmidt works at JKL Consulting in Stuttgart. Listen to these two phone calls she receives and say in which call ...**

a the caller gets through. ☐

b the caller leaves a message. ☐

c the caller gives his or her phone number. ☐

d Anke says she will ring back. ☐

e Anke says she will ask a colleague to ring back. ☐

Now listen again and write down the two messages.

VOCABULARY ASSISTANT

campaign *Kampagne*
deadline *Frist, Termin*
to mention *erwähnen*
to shift *verschieben*
suggestion *Vorschlag*
trade fair *Handelsmesse*

6 **Put these sentences from the first call into the right order, then listen again to check.**

1 afraid here I'm the isn't at moment Jonathan.
2 message like him leave would to a for you?
3 me pen get let a.
4 call Jonathan shall ask you back I to?
5 number he does your have?
6 gets I'll your make Jonathan message sure.

Now match the beginnings and endings of sentences from the second call, then listen to check.

a I'm calling about
b You said that
c You told me
d Can I call you back later today
e Can you give it to me again
f I'll talk to Henry and

☐ Henry was too busy to join the team.
☐ just in case?
☐ as soon as I've had the chance to speak to him?
☐ that we could take Maria instead.
☐ the email you sent me yesterday.
☐ call you straight back.

REFERRING TO PREVIOUS COMMUNICATION

Normally when we are calling someone back, we need to refer to previous communication like a phone call or an email to explain why we are calling. This can involve reporting or summarizing what another person has said. When we do this, we normally put tenses one step back 'into the past', as in the examples below.

"Sorry, I'm too busy."	*You said that you **were** too busy.*
*"I **was** ill on Monday."*	*She said that you **had been** ill on Monday.*

If the situation we are talking about is still true or relevant, however, we don't always change the tense.

*"I **can't** come to the meeting."*	*He said that he **can't** come to the meeting. OR*
	*He said that he **couldn't** come to the meeting.*
*"I'll **email** you asap."*	*She said that she'**ll email** me asap. OR*
	*She said that she **would email** me asap.*

We often use 'reporting verbs' like *ask*, *tell* and *mention* when we are reporting what someone said. Look at the examples below and notice how the verbs are used.

*"**Will** the 10th be OK for you?"*	*You **asked me if** the 10th would be OK for me.*
*"I **sent** the email on Monday."*	*She **told me that** she had sent the email on Monday.*
*"I'm **thinking** about going."*	*Jonathan **mentioned that** he was thinking about going.*

7 Complete the sentences below as in the example.

1 "The quality is too low."

They said *the quality was too low.*

2 "Maybe we can find another supplier."

She told me _____

3 "It will be difficult to schedule a new meeting."

He said _____

4 "Can you deliver earlier?"

They asked _____

5 "We hired two new employees."

You mentioned _____

6 "I'm going to the UK in June."

He told me _____

8 Complete the sentences using the prepositions from the box.

about • after • at • for • in • on • to • until

1 Unfortunately no one is available to take your call _____ the moment.

2 Please leave a message _____ the beep or send us a fax _____ 042 823 4421.

3 This is Adam Gray calling _____ Stefanie Renner.

4 I'm calling _____ the email you sent me yesterday.

5 Maybe you can get back _____ me.

6 I'll be _____ the office _____ 5 pm today if you want to call me.

9 **Use one word or phrase from each column to make eight sentences for dealing with messages.**

Can I	afraid	she	again just in case?
Can you	call	the email	back later today?
Could	calling about	you	for her?
Would you like	you get back	to me	gets your message.
I'm	please give me	your number	have my number already.
I'm	to leave	you	isn't here at the moment.
I'll	make sure	a message	on this asap, please?
I	think	she	you sent me yesterday.

a Can *I call you back later today?* _____

b Can you _____

c Could _____

d Would you like _____

e I'm _____

f I'm _____

g I'll _____

h I _____

Now use the sentences above to complete the dialogue extracts below.

A Sorry, I'm really busy at the moment. *Can I call you back later today?* _____ [1]

B Sure, no problem. I'll be in the office all afternoon.

A _____ [2]
   Is that right?

B Erm ... let me check. Hold on a second ... Yes, I have it here. 879 234 89.
   Is that right?

A Yes, that's right.

A I'm sorry, Martina isn't here at the moment. _____

_____ 3

B Yes please. I'd like to know the date of the next project meeting.

A OK. _____ 4

A It might be easier if she calls me. I'll be in the office until 3 pm today.

B OK. I think we've got your contact details, but _____

_____ 5

A Of course. It's 011 324 893 25.

A Can I speak to Beate Schulze, please?

B Oh, _____ 6 Can I

take a message?

Hi Patrice. This is Roland. _____ 7

There seems to be a problem with the schedule. _____

_____ 8

10 **Work with a partner to make two phone calls. Look at the useful phrases below before you look at your role cards.**

PARTNER FILES → File 05, p. 48
File 05, p. 50

USEFUL-PHRASES

Taking a message	**Leaving a message**
I'm afraid [name] isn't here at the moment.	This is [name]. I'm calling about ...
Would you like to leave a message for her/him?	[name] asked me to call her/him (back).
Let me just check (that) I've got that right.	I just wanted to check/confirm/ask if ...
Shall I tell [name] to call you back?	Could you ask her/him to call me back?
Does [name] have your number?	I'll be in the office today until ...
I'll make sure [name] gets your message.	
I'll tell him/let him know that you called.	

11 **Translate these sentences. Try to use expressions from this unit.**

1 Sie können mich unter 544 332 64 erreichen.
2 Kann ich ihr etwas ausrichten?
3 Eileen hat mich gebeten, sie zurückzurufen.
4 Hier ist Mary Lamb. Ich rufe wegen des Treffens an.
5 Er hat mir gesagt, dass er den Brief schon geschickt hat.

HANGING UP

Do you love answering machines and voicemail or hate them? Which opinion(s) do you agree with?

I don't really like answering machines that much, but I can see they can be useful sometimes. If I call someone and I get their answering machine, I normally hang up, think about what I want to say and then I ring back and leave the message. If it's in English, then I sometimes write the whole message out and get someone to check it before I call back.

Sometimes answering machines make difficult situations easier. It's much easier to say 'no' in an answering machine message than it is in a normal conversation. And answering machines mean I don't have to talk to people I don't like – I can just leave them a short message with the important information instead of speaking to them directly.

I hate talking to answering machines. I never know what to say, and I feel really self-conscious. Whenever I get someone's answering machine, I just hang up. I can call them back later if it's important.

I often end up playing 'telephone tag'. Someone calls me and leaves a message on my machine, then I call back and get their voicemail, then they call me and get my machine, and so on. Sometimes I have a whole conversation like that!

I think voicemail is great! If I don't want to be disturbed then I let the machine take my calls. If it's something important, I can call the person back. It's also a good way of screening my calls if I'm not sure I want to talk to the person who's calling.

OVER TO YOU

What do you think are the advantages and disadvantages of using answering machines and voicemail at work?

Do you ever play 'telephone tag' with business contacts?

What tips can you think of for using answering machines or voicemail effectively?

4

"When would suit you?"

PICKING UP

How well can you talk about times and dates in English? Try this quiz and compare your answers with a partner's. Then check your answers in the key.

1 Which of the time expressions are *not* possible in English?
  a   2 pm
  b   2 o'clock pm
  c   2 pm in the afternoon
  d   2 o'clock in the afternoon
  e   14 o'clock

2 How do you say the following expressions in English?
  a   *halb sieben*
  b   *kurz vor/nach*
  c   *Viertel vor/nach*
  d   *Mitternacht*
  e   *Mittag*

3 What does the date 01.02.06 mean to
  a   an American person?
  b   a British person?

4 Here are some ways to say the date '28 May 2005'. Which are not possible in English?
  a   the twenty-eighth of May, two thousand and five
  b   the twenty-eighth of May, two thousand five
  c   May twenty-eighth, two thousand and five
  d   the twenty-eighth May, two thousand and five
  e   the twenty-eight of May, two thousand and five

(Comic strip: Left panel — speech bubble "DAS IS KOMISCH. ER HAT HALB ZEHN GESAGT." with clock showing 9:35. Right panel — speech bubble "HOW STRANGE. SHE SAID HALF TEN." with clock showing 10:35.)

If you had trouble with this quiz, then go to page 68 for help with talking about dates and times!

go to page 68

19

1   Simon Mellor works at London Bank in Frankfurt. Look at his diary for next week, then listen and write in the appointment that he makes.

Monday

Tuesday
  9–5 KPMG meeting

Wednesday

Thursday   *4 pm telephone conference with US office*

Friday

Saturday

Sunday

British English	American English
diary	planner
mobile (phone)	cell (phone)
half (past) two	half past two

2 **Listen again and complete the table with suitable phrases from the dialogue.**

SUGGESTING A MEETING OR AN APPOINTMENT	SAYING IF A TIME IS CONVENIENT OR NOT
I was wondering if you might have time to meet me while I'm in town.	

ASKING ABOUT OR SUGGESTING A TIME TO MEET	
	CONFIRMING AN ARRANGEMENT

Now add these useful phrases to the table above.

Could we schedule a meeting for next month?

OK, so that's 2 pm in the conference room.

Yes, I'm free then.

What about Thursday?

Where would be the best place to meet?

Do you have time to meet tomorrow?

3 **Use phrases from your table to practise a dialogue with a partner.**

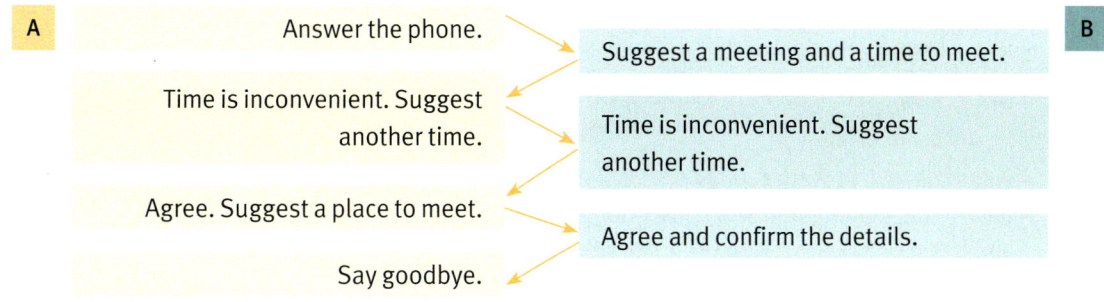

A
Answer the phone.

Time is inconvenient. Suggest another time.

Agree. Suggest a place to meet.

Say goodbye.

B
Suggest a meeting and a time to meet.

Time is inconvenient. Suggest another time.

Agree and confirm the details.

TALKING ABOUT ARRANGEMENTS

We usually use the present continuous with a 'future' time expression to talk about arrangements.

*I'm **flying** in on Monday morning.*
*And then I'm **having dinner** with my client in the evening.*

20

4 One of Alexa's clients in Frankfurt calls Hilary, Alexa's personal assistant. Look at the extract from Alexa's diary below and use the verbs in the box to complete the dialogue. Then listen to check your answer.

come (x2) • meet (x2) • have (x2) • fly

	Monday	Tuesday	Wednesday
7am			
8am	8.10 fly to Frankfurt		
9am			
10am			meeting with Simon
11am			
12am	meeting with Yves		
1pm	Gainsbourg	lunch with James Copeland	
2pm			meeting with Helmut
3pm			Fischer
4pm			
5pm			
6pm			6.45 fly to London
7pm	dinner with George		
8pm	(check)	dinner with Claire	
9pm			
10pm			

Hilary   JPL Consulting. Hilary Wilkins speaking.

Anna   Hello Hilary. This is Anna Roth from Frankfurt. Is Alexa there, please?

Hilary   I'm afraid she isn't. Can I help at all?

Anna   Well, a colleague told me that Alexa *is coming* [1] to Frankfurt next week. I'd like to see her while she's here, if she has time.

Hilary   Okay. Let me look at her schedule and we'll figure something out. When would suit you best?

Anna   I'm pretty flexible. Maybe you can tell me when she's free?

Hilary   Let me see. Okay, so she _____ [2] to Frankfurt first thing on Monday morning. Then she _____ [3] a client at 12. In the evening she _____ [4] dinner with a friend.

Anna   Hmm. Sounds like she's quite busy. What about Tuesday?

Hilary   Well, she's free on Tuesday morning. But then she _____ [5] lunch with a colleague at 1 and she _____ [6] someone in the evening.

Anna   Okay. And Wednesday?

Hilary   That's pretty full. She has a couple of meetings during the day then she _____ [7] back to London in the evening.

Anna   Okay. Well, maybe you can pencil me in on Tuesday morning. Say, 10 o'clock?

Hilary   10 o'clock on Tuesday. Okay, I'll double-check that with Alexa and send you a quick email to confirm the meeting.

Anna   Wonderful. Thanks for your help.

Hilary   You're welcome. Bye now.

Now work with a partner and ask each other about your appointments for this week or next week.

5   **Use in, on, at or Ø (= no preposition) to complete the time expressions.**

1 _on_ Monday

2 _Ø_ tomorrow

3 ____ the morning

4 ____ Friday morning

5 ____yesterday evening

6 ____ last night

7 ____ next week

8 ____ March 17th

9 ____ the weekend

10 ____ Christmas

11 ____ 10 o'clock

12 ____ midnight

13 ____ March

14 ____ 1990

15 ____ the evening

SMALL TALK

Normally when we call someone we know, we make a little bit of small talk before we start talking business. This is especially common if we are calling someone to make an arrangement.
Here are some typical telephone small talk questions.

How are things in [name of town] / at [name of firm]?
Are things busy with you?
What have you been up to? (=What have you been doing recently?)
How is the weather there?
Are you also having nice/terrible weather there?
How was your holiday/your trip to [name of place]?
How did the conference/trade fair go?
How is [name of husband/wife/partner]/are the kids?

Normally we mark the change from small talk to business with a signal word like **'listen'** or **'anyway'**, possibly followed by the name of the person we are talking to.

Listen *Frank, I was **actually** calling about …*
Anyway *Uta, I **actually** wanted to ask you if …*

Here 'actually' shows that we are changing the topic. (See unit 1 for more information on 'actually'.)

---

6   **Match the small talk questions to the answers.**

1   How are things in Paris?

2   How's the weather in Glasgow?

3   How was your holiday in Spain?

4   How are the kids?

5   What have you been up to?

6   Are things busy with you?

a   Nothing much, apart from work, to be honest. It's been really hectic here.

b   Very well, thanks. The oldest one has just started school.

c   Wet, as usual!

d   It's not too bad, actually. Last month was a nightmare, though.

e   Very nice. We had a great time.

f   Oh, you know what it's like. Same old thing as always.

7 Work with a partner. First write down three 'small talk' questions. (Try to make them relevant to the other person.) Then follow the steps below to make a phone call. Remember to use signal words like *so* and *well* to show when you want to move from one stage of the conversation to the next.

A		B
Answer the phone.	→	Say hello. Say your name.
Respond. Ask small talk question.	←	
	→	Respond. Ask small talk question.
Respond. Ask follow-up question (if appropriate).	←	
	→	Respond. Start talking about business.

21

8 It's now Monday morning and Alexa is calling Simon's personal assistant, Thorsten Hofmeister. Tick the sentences you hear.

1 I'm afraid something has come up. ☐
2 I'm afraid I have to reschedule our appointment. ☐
3 One of my clients has cancelled our appointment … ☐
4 One of my clients has brought forward our appointment … ☐
5 So I wanted to ask Simon if we could meet a bit earlier … ☐
6 So I wanted to ask Simon if we could postpone our meeting … ☐
7 Just let me know if there are any more changes. ☐
8 Just give me a call if there are any more changes. ☐

Simon – Alexa Johnston called

Listen again and complete Thorsten's message for Simon.

CHANGING AN ARRANGEMENT

If you want to change an arrangement, it's polite to give a concrete reason for doing so.

> *I'm afraid something has come up. One of my clients has brought forward our appointment.*

The phrase 'something has come up' means that something unexpected has happened and it's probably not something you can control. Notice that the present perfect tense (*has come up/has brought forward*) is often used in this context (ie, for giving news) to talk about something that happened in the past and has an effect on the present.

English speakers are often extra polite when suggesting something that might be inconvenient for the other person. Here are some typical ways to suggest or ask about changing an arrangement.

> *So **I wanted to ask you if** we could meet **a bit** earlier in the morning.*
> *I **was wondering if** we could reschedule our appointment.*
> ***Could** we **possibly** postpone the presentation?*
> ***Would it be possible** to meet a bit later?*

9 **Complete the sentences below with words from the box.**

> bit • changed • delayed • lasted • missed • possible •
> possibly • postponed • wanted • wondering

1 I was _____ if we could meet on Friday instead. My client has _____ our schedule.

2 I _____ to ask if we could meet tomorrow instead of today. I've _____ my flight and I'm afraid I'm going to arrive very late.

3 Could we _____ cancel our appointment? My meeting _____ longer than expected.

4 Could we meet a _____ later? I'm afraid my customer has _____ our meeting.

5 Would it be _____ to reschedule our meeting? My train has been _____ .

10 **It is now 8.50 am on Tuesday morning and Alexa is calling Simon again. Listen to the conversation. Why is Alexa calling?**

22

Listen again and complete the phrases.

I'm actually still _____[1] for the train so I'm afraid I _____[2] be a few minutes late.

Sorry, you're _____[3] up a little. I didn't _____[4] that last part.

I'll see you when I _____[5] you.

I should be there by 9.15 at the _____[6], but I'll call you again if there are any more _____[7].

I think I'm _____[8] the connection. I'd _____[9] go.

11 **Look at these phrases which are typical for mobile phone calls. Match the questions to the answers. (Sometimes more than one answer is possible.)**

1 Where are you?

2 Is this a good time to talk?

3 Have you got a couple of minutes?

4 Can you hear me?

5 Are you still there?

6 What was that beeping noise?

a You're breaking up a little. Would you like to try calling me again later?

b Yes, I am. I just lost the connection for a second.

c I'm on the train.

d I'm afraid I'm in a meeting at the moment. Can we talk later?

e Sure. What can I do for you?

f My battery's low – we might get cut off, I'm afraid.

g Not really, I'm afraid. Can I call you back later?

h I'm actually in the office. You can call me on my landline if you like.

12 Complete the sentences with the correct form of the words in the box.

> appointment • arrangements • date (x2) • arrange • cancel •
> postpone • bring forward

1 What's the _____ today? Is it the 17th of March?

2 Unfortunately I have to _____ the meeting. I can't find a time when we can all meet.

3 I have a(n) _____ to see Ms Fraser.

4 They told me that the conference room is already booked for 2 pm and asked if we could _____ the meeting to 10 am. Is that OK for you?

5 The department secretary made all the _____ for my trip.

6 I have a(n) _____ with the new guy in purchasing tonight. We're going to see the new Tarantino movie.

7 It seems like a lot of people are ill or on holiday this week. Why don't we _____ the presentation until next week?

8 I'm calling to _____ a time to meet next week.

13 Work with a partner to make three phone calls. First look at the list of useful phrases on this page. Then look at your 'diary' and the instructions in the partner files.

PARTNER FILES → File 06, p. 49
File 06, p. 51

USEFUL PHRASES

Making an arrangement
I was wondering if you might have time to meet next week.
What day/When would you suit you?
Can we fix a meeting for Tuesday?
How about Monday morning?
Shall we say 9 o'clock at my office?

Changing an appointment
I'm calling about our appointment.
I'm afraid something has come up.
I wanted to ask you if we could postpone/bring forward our meeting.
Could we possibly reschedule/cancel our appointment?

Saying you will be late
I'm afraid my meeting has taken longer than I expected.
I might be a few minutes late.
I should be there by 3.15 at the latest, but I'll call you again if there are any more delays.

14 Translate these sentences. Try to use expressions from this unit.

1 Leider ist etwas dazwischengekommen.
2 Sie hat einen Termin mit der Geschäftsführerin.
3 Ich komme eventuell ein paar Minuten zu spät.
4 Ich fliege am Samstag nach New York.
5 Ich habe den ganzen Tag zu tun.
6 Ich glaube, ich habe Mittwochnachmittag Zeit.

Have mobile phones made our lives easier or are they just annoying and unnecessary? Which opinion(s) do you agree with?

> I hate mobile phones. I think they're one of the most annoying inventions ever. And people make so many pointless phone calls now. Like if you're meeting someone, it used to be that you just arranged a time and then met at that time and place. Now everyone feels that they have to phone twenty times before the meeting to say they're going to be five minutes late, or to change the time, or whatever.

> My mobile phone has made my life much easier. Now I never need to worry about being late for an appointment; if I'm stuck in traffic, I just call and let the person know.

> Mobile phones can be useful, but I don't like the fact that people can always contact me. Sometimes I just want to be left alone!

> I wish people would be more considerate and switch their phones off when they don't need them. And I don't know why people feel they always need to answer their phone if it rings during a meeting or at the cinema. Surely they can let their voicemail pick up and then listen to any messages later.

OVER TO YOU

What do you think should be the rules of mobile phone etiquette? Make a list of do's and don'ts and discuss it with the class.

5

"I'm very sorry about that."

PICKING UP

What are your attitudes to complaints?
Make a cross on the scale to represent how much you agree (5 = I agree 100 %) or disagree
(0 = I disagree 100 %).

	agree			disagree		
1 I never apologize for a mistake someone else makes.	5	4	3	2	1	0
2 You should always accept responsibility for a problem if a customer makes a complaint.	5	4	3	2	1	0
3 I don't like complaining; normally I accept bad service without saying anything.	5	4	3	2	1	0
4 If someone calls me with a complaint, I try to listen carefully.	5	4	3	2	1	0
5 I always try to find a colleague who can solve the problem if I can't do it myself.	5	4	3	2	1	0
6 Some people just enjoy complaining; I don't think you have to take every complaint seriously.	5	4	3	2	1	0
7 Customer complaints can help us improve our service.	5	4	3	2	1	0

"IF YOU ARE CALLING WITH A COMPLAINT, PRESS 3 & A MACHINE WILL LISTEN SYMPATHETICALLY TO YOUR PROBLEM"

Discuss your answers with a partner.

1   **Listen to the four short extracts from phone calls. In which call does the person called ...**

23-26

a   deal with the problem immediately? ☐   c   connect the caller to the person responsible? ☐
b   tell the caller to call another number? ☐   d   promise to call the caller back? ☐

In which conversation do you hear the following phrases?

A   Let me put you through to our accounts department. [7]
B   You seem to have forgotten the attachment. ☐
C   Unfortunately I can't put you through directly, but let me give you the number. ☐
D   Can I check that and call you back? ☐
E   I'll send you the file right away. ☐
F   You actually need to speak to our technical support hotline. ☐
G   There appears to be a mistake on the invoice you sent us. ☐
H   Some of the components don't seem to work. ☐

2 **Listen to the conversation and take notes. What is the problem and how will Reva deal with it?**

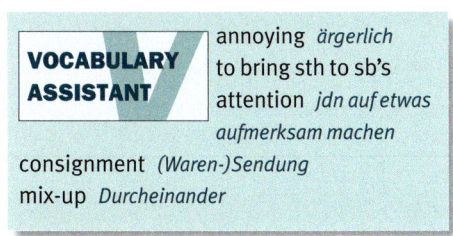

VOCABULARY ASSISTANT

annoying *ärgerlich*
to bring sth to sb's attention *jdn auf etwas aufmerksam machen*
consignment *(Waren-)Sendung*
mix-up *Durcheinander*

After the calls, Reva writes an email to his boss about the problem. Use your notes (and listen again if necessary) to complete the email.

Delete   Reply   Reply All   Forward   Print

From: Reva Burgos   **To:** Paula Kilroy
CC: **Subject:** Delivery problem

Hi Paula,

Just to let you know, I got a call from Abby Dickson from Syke Electronics today. She told me that there was

a problem with the latest _____ [1] we sent them. Apparently, some of the _____ [2] we

sent them contained the wrong _____ [3] model. (They ordered the _____ [4] sensor,

but we sent the _____ [5] model instead.)

I told Abby I would send her the correct units by _____ [6] delivery with _____ [7]

Logistics. The logistics company will _____ [8] the other units up when they deliver the correct units.

Best wishes,
Reva

---

3 **Listen again and find the missing words.**

1   There _____ to be a small problem with your latest consignment.

2   Oh dear. I'm _____ to hear that.

3   What's the problem _____ ?

4   I'll _____ on to this problem immediately.

5   Well, _____ is what I'm going to do.

6   Thanks for _____ that out, Reva.

7   Again, I'm really sorry about the _____ .

8   I'll _____ make sure it doesn't happen again.

Now decide which of the sentences above you can use to do the following.

describe a problem   *1*   apologize _____
clarify what the problem is _____   say how you will solve the problem _____

COMPLAINING

Normally we explain the context before we describe our complaint in detail.

I'm calling/I have a question about the invoice you sent us.

In addition to 'I'm afraid' and 'unfortunately', we often use verbs like 'seem' and 'appear' to describe the problem. These verbs make the complaint sound less aggressive and allow the possibility that we might be wrong.

I'm afraid there's a slight problem with the goods you sent us.
Unfortunately it seems we haven't received the shipment.
It seems you forgot the attachment (OR: You seem to have forgotten the attachment.)
There appears to be a small problem with your latest consignment.

Similarly, we often say 'a small / slight / bit of a problem' even when the problem is big. To native speakers of English, the sentence 'There's a big problem …' (even if true) sounds aggressive and impolite.

4   **Rewrite these sentences to make them more polite. Use the words in brackets.**

1   The parts you sent us don't work. (seem)   *The parts you sent us don't seem to work.* _____

2   You delivered the consignment to the wrong address. (unfortunately) _____

   _____

3   The total on the bill is wrong. (appears) _____

4   We have a problem with the equipment you sold us. (afraid/slight) _____

   _____

5   You sent us the wrong model. (seem) _____

6   You gave us the incorrect information. (unfortunately) _____

   _____

APOLOGIZING

There are different phrases you can use to apologize, for example:

I'm sorry about …
I'd like to apologize for … (more formal)
Please accept my/our apologies for … (very formal)

You can use words like 'really', 'very' and 'extremely' or the expression 'I have to say' to make an apology stronger.

I'm very/extremely sorry about this.
I have to say I'm really very sorry about this.

If the mistake really is your (or your company's) fault, you can admit this by saying:

That's entirely our fault.
There must have been a mix-up.

SOLVING THE PROBLEM

Customers also appreciate it if you take responsibility for solving the problem. Here we often use the *will* future when we promise to do something (often spontaneously).

I'll get on to that problem immediately.
I'll make sure it gets sorted out straight away.
I'll personally make sure it doesn't happen again.

If you don't want to make such a firm promise, you can use 'should' instead.

You should have them first thing tomorrow morning.
You should have it by Friday at the latest.

5 **Complete the two phone calls with words and phrases from the box.**

> sorry again about the mix-up • 'll make sure that gets sorted out •
> it seems you sent us • there appears to be a mistake •
> please accept my apologies • I'm really sorry about • could you tell me

Etta   I'm calling about the business cards you did for us. _____
_____¹ with the address.

Tania   Oh no. I'm very sorry to hear that. _____² what the
mistake is exactly?

Etta   Well, you've printed the company address as one word, but it's actually two words.

Tania   _____³ for the mistake. That's entirely our fault.
_____⁴ straight away and we'll send you new
cards as soon as we can.

Etta   That sounds good. Thanks for your help.

• • • • • • •

Erich   This is Erich Kessler from Fatima Networks. I'm calling about the software release you sent us
yesterday.

Basil   Uh huh. Is everything okay with it?

Erich   Actually, no. _____⁵ the old version. The disk has
version 2.2 on it, not 2.3.

Basil   Oh dear. _____⁶ that. I'll send you a new disk straight
away. You should get it first thing tomorrow.

Erich   That sounds good, thanks. I'll probably call you again when it arrives.

Basil   Do that. And _____⁷.

Erich   No problem.

Which conversation is more formal, and which is more informal?

6 **Complete the sentences 1–5 with *will* and the verbs in the box.**

> deliver • give • make sure • send

1   I *'ll send* _____ you the document straight away.
2   Don't worry. You _____ the goods by lunchtime tomorrow.
3   I _____ personally _____ it doesn't happen again.
4   We _____ you ten units free, by way of compensation.
5   The package is on its way. They _____ it by 5 pm today.

7 **Work with a partner to practise the following dialogue.**

| A | Say you have a problem. | → | Ask what the problem is. | B |

Explain the problem. → Admit responsibility and apologize.
Say what you will do to solve the problem.

Thank your partner. → Apologize again and say goodbye.

8 **Listen to the call to a technical support hotline and make notes to complete the form.**

Nexus Retail Systems	I	Technical Support
Call record		
1 Name of caller		
2 Company		
3 Description of problem		
4 Action taken		

9 **Listen to the call again and complete the phrases.**

1 Are you the _____ person to talk to?

2 Could you explain the problem in more _____ ?

3 I'm going to need some more _____ to solve the problem.

4 In that _____ , it must be the ink cartridge.

5 If you have any _____ just give me a _____ .

6 My name's Anja Schneider, but you can speak to _____ of our operatives here on the hotline.

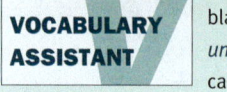
VOCABULARY ASSISTANT

blank *leer, unbedruckt* cash register *Kasse* gradually *allmählich* ink cartridge *Tintenpatrone* operative (Call-Center) *Mitarbeiter/in* receipt *Quittung, Bon* suddenly *plötzlich*

10 **Work with a partner to make the following two phone calls. Look at the useful phrases before going to the partner files.**

PARTNER FILES → File 07, p. 49
File 07, p. 51

USEFUL PHRASES

Explaining a problem
There seems/appears to be a problem with ...
I'm afraid there's a problem with ...
Unfortunately, you/we ...

Explaining what you will do
This is what I'm going to do.
I'll send/revise/prepare ...
I'll make sure it doesn't happen again.

Apologizing
I'm (really) (very) sorry about that.
I have to say I'm extremely sorry about this.
Please accept my apologies.

11 Translate these sentences. Try to use expressions from this unit.

1 Es scheint ein kleines Problem mit der Rechnung zu geben.
2 Das ist wirklich ärgerlich.
3 Die Sendung müssten gleich morgen früh bei Ihnen sein.
4 Vielen Dank, dass Sie sich darum gekümmert haben.
5 Ich verspreche, dass so etwas nicht noch einmal passiert.

Read this article from a customer care magazine and answer the questions.

DEALING WITH COMPLAINTS

Dealing well with complaints shows how important customer care is for your company. It shows that you listen to your customers, that you want to learn from your mistakes and that you are continually trying to improve your services.

Below are some tips for dealing with complaints.

✔ **TAKE EACH COMPLAINT SERIOUSLY**

If you deal with a complaint in the wrong way, one unhappy customer may tell many more people about your poor service. On the other hand, if you deal with a complaint successfully, that customer will probably do business with you again. Remember that finding new customers is much more expensive than keeping current ones.

✔ **LISTEN TO YOUR CUSTOMERS AND SHOW THEM YOU UNDERSTAND WHAT THEY ARE FEELING**

Listen carefully to your callers and let them get rid of their anger or frustration. Try to see things from their point of view and make sure you show them that you understand their problem.

✔ **ADMIT THAT A MISTAKE HAS BEEN MADE AND SAY SORRY**

If the customer thinks something is a complaint, then it is, even if you think the problem is not important. If your company has really made a mistake, say so and apologize. Even if you think a mistake has not been made, show the customer that you understand the problem. Never tell the customer that the complaint is not important.

✔ **ACCEPT PERSONAL RESPONSIBILITY**

Even if you are not directly responsible for the mistake, it is not important for the customer whose fault it really is. You are the face of your organization and it is your responsibility to solve the problem. If you are not able to do so yourself, find the person who can. Make sure you support the customer until the right person can help.

✔ **TAKE IMMEDIATE ACTION**

Customers want their problems solved quickly. Acting fast shows customers that you take them and their problems seriously.

✔ **OFFER COMPENSATION**

If possible, try to compensate customers for a mistake, e.g. by giving a small discount. Often the fact that you are giving some kind of compensation is more important than the compensation itself.

✔ **THANK THE CUSTOMER FOR MAKING THE COMPLAINT**

This may sound illogical, but complaints are the best feedback you can get. They show how you can improve your service and make your customers more satisfied.

OVER TO YOU

Look back at the telephone calls in this unit. Do the people follow the advice given above?
Does your company handle complaints well? How could it improve its complaints procedure?
Think of a complaint you have made to another company. What was it? Was it dealt with?

6

"How does that sound?"

SO WE'VE AGREED WE'D LIKE TO MEET FOR A DRINK. WHAT SORT OF TIME FRAME WERE YOU THINKING OF?

IT'S DIFFICULT TO SAY AT THIS STAGE, BUT I COULD TENTATIVELY SUGGEST 7 PM...

PICKING UP

Work with a partner. Answer the questions first for yourself, then interview your partner and make a note of his or her answers.

	YOU	YOUR PARTNER
What kind of things do you make agreements about (eg prices, delivery times, conditions)?		
How often do you make agreements on the telephone?		
What problems do you have when discussing business on the telephone?		
Give an example of a successful (or an unsuccessful) agreement you have made on the telephone.		

29

1 **Wolfgang Zimmer works for a small company in Cologne. He's calling a British supplier about a possible order and to get details about delivery times and prices. Listen and complete his notes.**

> Possible supplier: _____ [1] Semiconductors
> Order _____ [2] chips from them?
> We need chips by the _____ [3] of next month at the latest.
> Possible solution: introduce _____ [4] at the factory
> Problem: would be more expensive – _____ [5] to
> _____ [6] per cent?
> They will send _____ [7] by email, then we can talk again
> tomorrow.

VOCABULARY ASSISTANT

ballpark figure *grobe Schätzung*   feasible *machbar*   to place an order *einen Auftrag erteilen*   quotation *Kostenvoranschlag*   shift work *Schichtarbeit*   tight schedule *enger Zeitplan*   urgently *dringend*

2 **Match the sentence beginnings (1–6) and endings (a–f) to make sentences from the dialogue, then listen again to check.**

1 We need them
2 We really need them by then
3 If you weren't able to deliver by then,
4 However, if we introduced shift work at the factory,
5 Would you be prepared to pay more for the chips
6 Well, that sounds like

a if we're going to meet our project deadlines with our customer.
b then we would probably be able to manufacture the chips faster.
c in order to get them faster?
d by the middle of next month at the latest.
e it would be feasible.
f we would have to go to another supplier.

TALKING ABOUT POSSIBILITIES

When negotiating, it is common to use conditional forms like the ones below to show that we are talking about possibilities.

> **Would you be** prepared to pay more for the chips in order to get them faster?
> **If you weren't able to** deliver by then, we **would have to** go to another supplier.
> **If we introduced** shift work at the factory, **then we could manufacture** the chips faster.

Note that in *if*-sentences the simple past form of the verb (and not 'would') is used in the 'if' part of the sentence.

> If we **introduced** shift work at the factory, then we could manufacture the chips faster.
> NOT: ~~If we would introduce ...~~

---

3 **Complete the conference call dialogue using the correct form of the words in brackets. Use could or would where appropriate. Sometimes more than one answer is possible.**

A ... OK, so the next point is our British office. It's far too expensive and we urgently need to reduce our costs. Do any of you have ideas how we _could do_ [1] (do) that?

B Well, if they _moved_ [2] (move) into a smaller office, we _would save_ [3] (save) a lot of money on rent.

A Yes, but the move itself _____ [4] (cost) a lot of money. And it _____ _____ [5] (cause) a lot of disruptions to our business.

C What if we _____ [6] (reduce) the number of staff?

B That _____ [7] (cause) a lot of bad feeling among the rest of the staff. And paying people off _____ [8] (be) expensive.

C What about if we _____ [9] (ask) them to work from home? Most of the time they're travelling anyway. Then we _____ [11] (rent) out that office space to other people.

A That _____ [12] (work). Let me think about it ...

HEDGES

Hedges (phrases which express doubt or make a statement sound less certain) are useful when making suggestions or tentatively agreeing to something. Native speakers of English often use words like 'probably' and 'might' or expressions like 'I would say' and 'I think I can provisionally say' when trying to reach an agreement.

> We could **probably** work with that.
> We **might** be able to work with that.
> **I would say** (it would be) between 5 to 10 per cent more expensive.
> **I think I can provisionally say** that we could work with that.

Note that the use of hedges is more common in British English than American English.

---

4 **Rewrite the sentences to make them more tentative, using the words given. Sometimes more than one answer is possible.**

1 We can give you a discount. (provisionally) *I think I can provisionally say that we will be able to give you a discount.*

2 We can deliver by the end of the week. (might) _____

3 We can solve the problem. (would) _____

4 It will be difficult. (probably) _____

5 We can change the specifications of the product. (provisionally) _____

_____

5 **Viktor Klein is calling a supplier to negotiate some prices. Listen and complete the email.**

Hi Alex

Just wanted to let you know that I've spoken to Francesca _____[1] at Hineman Pharmaceuticals about the saline solution order. You remember there was a problem with their _____[2], which was roughly _____[3] higher than the competition. I asked if there was any chance of a _____[4], and they said they can give us a _____[5] reduction on orders over _____[6] cases. I said I would check with you, then contact them if we want to place the order.

Let me know what you think.

Regards
Viktor

VOCABULARY ASSISTANT	case hier: *Kiste* to compare *vergleichen*
	competition *Konkurrenz* discount *Rabatt*
	to expect *erwarten* saline solution *Salzlösung*

6 Now listen again and complete the gaps with the words and phrases you hear.

Viktor   I'm calling because I wanted to _____¹ our conversation from yesterday.

Francesca   That's right. You said you wanted to compare products and prices from different

             suppliers, _____²?

             · · · · · · · · · · ·

Francesca   Wonderful. Shall I fax you the order form? We could …

Viktor   Sorry, can I _____³ you there? There's actually one small problem.

             · · · · · · · · · · ·

Francesca   Well yes, that _____⁴, but I think you'll find our quality is higher and …

Viktor   Yes, yes, but can I just say _____⁵? I wanted to ask …

TURN-TAKING

It can be difficult on the telephone to know when to speak yourself and when to let your partner speak. Since you and the person you're talking to can't see each other, you have to use verbal instead of non-verbal techniques instead. Here are some suggestions.

- Ask questions and use question tags to show your partner that it's his or her turn to speak.

  Questions   **Question tags**
  How does that sound?   *You'll be in the office tomorrow, **won't you**?*
  What do you think?   *You said you wanted to compare prices, **didn't you**?*
  Is that OK?

- Avoid silences – they can make the person you're talking to feel uncomfortable. (See the ***Active listening strategies*** box on page 14 for more advice.)
- Use the following phrases to interrupt politely if your partner won't let you speak.

Yes, yes, but	
Sure, but	*can I just say something*
Sorry, (but)	*can I interrupt you there (for a second)?*
Of course, but	*can I stop you there?*

---

7 Work with a partner. First of all, think of something that you have to discuss on the telephone (eg a price, a delivery date, a project deadline). Then work with your partner to practise the dialogue below. Note: both partners should talk without stopping, so the other person has to (politely) interrupt!

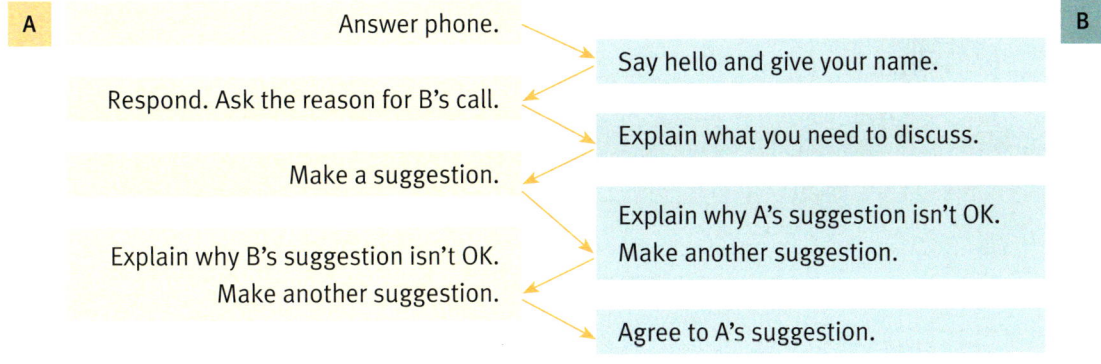

A	B
	Answer phone.
	Say hello and give your name.
Respond. Ask the reason for B's call.	
	Explain what you need to discuss.
Make a suggestion.	
	Explain why A's suggestion isn't OK. Make another suggestion.
Explain why B's suggestion isn't OK. Make another suggestion.	
	Agree to A's suggestion.

8 There are certain phrases which are often used when negotiating. Match the English expressions to the German translations.

1	to follow up our conversation	a	*grobe Schätzung*
2	room to manoeuvre	b	*ein enger Zeitplan*
3	a tight schedule	c	*einen Kostenvoranschlag erstellen*
4	to meet a deadline	d	*aus dem Stand/dem Stehgreif*
5	time frame	e	*das ist schwer zu sagen*
6	that depends	f	*einen Termin einhalten*
7	that's difficult to say	g	*um an unser Gespräch anzuknüpfen*
8	a ballpark figure	h	*(Handlungs-)Spielraum*
9	off the top of my head	i	*Zeitrahmen*
10	to prepare a quotation	j	*es kommt darauf an*

9 Now complete the mini-dialogues using the phrases above. (You may need to change the form of the expressions slightly.)

A Hello Fred. What can I do for you?

B I'm actually calling to _____[1] from yesterday.

A Why do you want to change the delivery date?

B We have a very _____[2] on this project. If we don't get the goods by next week, we won't _____[3] we agreed with our customer.

A Would you be prepared to pay more for higher quality?

B _____[4]. I would need to talk to my boss about that.

A What sort of _____[5] were you thinking about for the project? I mean, when would you need our services exactly?

B _____[6] at the moment. We haven't made any decisions yet.

A I can't say exactly how much it would cost.

B Well, can you give me a _____[7]?

A Sorry, I would need to check the spreadsheet. I can't give you an answer _____[8].

A Well, I'm pleased that we managed to reach an agreement.

B Me too. So, I'll _____[9] and send it to you by email later today.

A Can you give us a discount?

B I'm afraid we don't have much _____[10] on price.

10   **Work with a partner to do the following role-play. Read through the useful phrases before looking at your file.**

PARTNER FILES   ➜   File 08, p. 49
File 08, p. 51

USEFUL PHRASES

Making proposals	**Reacting to proposals**
I wanted to ask if there was any possibility of …	That sounds like it would be feasible.
Would you be prepared to …?	That sounds reasonable.
What if we …?	That depends.
	I don't think that would be possible.

---

11   **Translate these sentences. Try to use expressions from this unit.**

1   Es würde mich freuen, wenn es zu einer Zusammenarbeit käme.

2   Das klingt vernünftig.

3   Aus dem Stand kann ich das nicht einschätzen.

4   Dürfte ich Sie hier kurz unterbrechen?

5   Können wir diesem Termin einhalten? – Das kommt ganz darauf an.

Look at what these people say about negotiating over the telephone. Which opinion(s) do you agree with?

With some of my business contacts, I only speak to them on the telephone – we never meet face to face. That makes it more of a challenge when you need to reach agreements on things. That's one reason why I always try to make small talk before we discuss business. I find small talk helps to build a personal relationship and makes discussions easier.

I find it easier to discuss things face to face than on the telephone. You can't see the other person, so it's difficult to know exactly what they are thinking. There's no body language to help you and if the other person is silent it can mean different things. Maybe they are angry with you, or maybe they are just thinking about what you have said. It's difficult to tell.

Before I make a phone call where I have to negotiate something, I think about what I want exactly. What is the minimum I am prepared to accept? What is my best alternative if we don't manage to reach an agreement? That way I know before I begin how much room to manoeuvre I have.

I don't enjoy trying to reach agreements on the telephone. I find it difficult to say no to people and to stand up for what I want. Often I hang up the phone and am not happy with the agreement I've made, but then it's too late to change anything.

OVER TO YOU

What are your strategies for reaching agreements on the telephone?

How is discussing business on the telephone different from meeting face to face, in your opinion?

What could you personally do to improve your telephone negotiating skills?

Test yourself!

See how much you've learned about telephoning in English.
Use the clues to complete the crossword puzzle.

Across

6   What's the preposition? *How ... Wednesday morning?*

7   'für alle Fälle' (3 words): *Can you give me your number again, ... ?*

8   What's the preposition? *I'm tied ... all day.*

10 'buchstabieren': *Would you like me to ... that for you?*

13 'klingen': *How does that ... ?*

14 Another word for 'phoning': *My name is John Ellis. I'm ... from Retex Plc.*

15 'sicher stellen' (2 words): *I'll ... she gets your message.*

19 Another word for 'answerphone' (2 words): *I left a message on your ... .*

23 Another word for 'said': *Jonathan ... that he was going to the trade fair.*

28 'sonst': *Just let me know if there's anything ... I can do for you.*

29 What's the preposition? *I have a question ... your products.*

31 What's the preposition? *Let me read that ... to you.*

32 'dringend': *We need the parts very ... .*

33 Another word for 'busy': *I'm afraid Fred's line is ... .*

34 Another word for 'understand': *Sorry, I didn't ... that.*

Down

1   'grobe Schätzung' (2 words): *Can you give me a ... ?*

2   A way to apologize: *I'll personally make sure it doesn't ... again.*

3   'eigentlich': *I ... wanted to speak to Maria.*

4   The opposite of 'postpone' (2 words): *Unfortunately my client had to ... our meeting.*

5   'passen': *When would ... you?*

9   *Sorry, I'm not here at the moment. Please leave a ... after the tone.*

10 'sollte': *I think that ... be possible.*

11 'Durchwahl': *Shall I give you her ... number?*

12 'wollte': *I ... to ask you if you have time to meet.*

16 'begrüßen': *I ... your help.*

17 Another word for 'seems': *There ... to be a mistake on the invoice you sent us.*

18 *Monday at 3? Let me just check my ... .*

20 'falsch': *I think you have the ... number.*

21 A possible answer to this question: *How are you? – Can't ... .*

22 'bis': *I'll be in the office ... about 5pm today.*

24 Another word for 'pleased': *I'm ... to hear that.*

25 'unterbrechen': *Sorry, can I ... you there?*

26 What's the preposition? *Shall I put you ... to her?*

27 'sofort': *I'll talk to my boss and then I'll call you ... back.*

28 'genau': *What's the problem ... ?*

30 What's the preposition? *It's about our meeting. Something has come ... .*

Partner A | **Partner files**

Unit 1, Exercise 11   File 01

Call 1

Your name is Christine/Chris Fraser. It's 10 o'clock: time to make your phone calls. (You have a meeting from 12 until 5 pm.) Your first call is to NeuBau GmbH. You want to speak to your business contact there, Tanja Steinmann. You often call the company, so you have spoken to Tanja's PA (personal assistant) Alex several times before.

Call 2

Your name is Martin/Martina König. You work for Jasta-Karling as a secretary. Answer the phone and help the caller. Important: your boss, Karsten Böse, has told you that he doesn't want any phone calls today.

Unit 2, Exercise 7   File 02

First spell the place names below (1–4) for your partner. (The words in brackets tell you where you can find these places – they do exist!)

1   Ambato Finandrahana (Madagascar)
2   Narvskoye Vodokhranilishche (Estonia)
3   Thabana-Ntlenyana (Lesotho)
4   Lubuklinggau (Indonesia)

Then write down the words your partner spells for you (5–8).

5   _____
6   _____
7   _____
8   _____

Finally, spell the words 5–8 back to your partner to check your spelling. Did you get it right?

Unit 2, Exercise 10   File 03

Call 1

You work for RFM Electronics. Someone will call and ask about prices and telephone numbers. Look at these extracts from your current price list and internal telephone list and give them the information they need. (The price list is also available on your website www.rfm-electronics.com.)

6M138	**Optocoupler**	£0.70
6N148	**Optocoupler**	£0.90
UGN3505W	**Magnetic Sensor**	£4.00
74AC695	**Transceiver**	£1.30
75AC965	**Transceiver**	£1.85
TD2002V	**Audio Amplifier**	£5.40
PIC-101SCL IR	**Receiver Module**	£3.00
Potentiometer Thumbwheel 20K		£1.45

Marketing department	+44 193 221 6760 40
Production department	+44 193 221 6760 50
Quality department	+44 193 221 6760 60
Customer service department	+44 193 221 6760 70
Purchasing department	+44 193 221 6760 80

Call 2

You work for BrightFuture Pharmaceuticals. You have received an order from NDL Inc. but you don't have a delivery address. Call NDL Inc. to get the information. You would also like the email address and mobile phone number of the person who placed the order in case you have any more questions.

Unit 3, Exercise 4   File 04

Call 1

You are Monica Thompson's answering machine! Prepare a message saying that you are not here and asking the caller to leave a message after the beep. Read it out to the caller. Then listen and make a note of the caller's message.

Call 2

You are Monica Thompson. Phone the caller back and leave a message on his voicemail, thanking him for his help. You are also interested in talking to him about a new project – ask him if he can call you back some time this week.

Unit 3, Exercise 10   File 05

Call 1
Your name is Jay/Jill Thurber and you work for Soncha Engineering. Your colleague Gina Wilson is out of the office at the moment. Someone will call and ask for her. Take a message, checking all the details to make sure you understand them.

Call 2
Your name is Delmar/Dagmar Wagner and you work for HSF Banking Services. Your customer Sal Larkin from Bernes Insurance left a message for you, asking if you could meet him next week to talk about his company's investments. Call him and arrange a meeting. (You are free all day on Monday and Wednesday, and on Thursday morning.)
Here is your business card with your phone numbers in case you have to leave a message.

HSF Banking Services
Key Account Manager
Tel (office): 0044 20 3489 2142
Tel (mobile): 0044 79 234 8234
Email: d.wagner@hsf-banking.co.uk

Unit 4, Exercise 13   File 06

Each box represents one hour – the yellow boxes are when you are busy. Write appointments in the yellow boxes. Think of appointments which are realistic for you, for example a meeting with a client, a sales presentation, dinner with a business partner. Then role-play the three telephone conversations with your partner.

	Monday	Tuesday	Wednesday	Thursday	Friday
9 am					
10 am					
11 am					
12 noon					
1 pm					
2 pm					
3 pm					
4 pm					

Call 1
You want to meet your partner next week. You need at least two hours for the meeting. Call your partner and find a time when you are both free. (Remember that you are busy at the times marked by the yellow boxes.)

Call 2
Your partner will call you about the appointment.

Call 3
Your last meeting went on longer than you expected, and you are going to be late for your appointment with your partner. Call him/her on your mobile phone and let him/her know.

Unit 5, Exercise 10   File 07

Call 1
While you were on a business trip to the UK last week you hired a rental car from Easy Auto. You have just received the bill and found a mistake. Call Easy Auto and complain.

Easy Auto

Invoice

Car rented	Number of days	Price per day	Total
Volkswagen Passat	③ *2 days, not 3!*	£55	£165

Call 2
You work for a British translation agency called TransFast. A customer will call you to make a complaint. Deal with the complaint as politely and efficiently as you can. Note: you are only responsible for English/French translations, so problems with other languages are not your fault!

Unit 6, Exercise 10   File 08

You work for the German subsidiary of Gilee and Soare, an American multi-national accounting firm. You are currently in charge of a three-person team which is doing an audit on a large German company. However the work is taking longer than you expected and you think you will need one more person on the team if you are going to meet the deadline for the work. It is time for your weekly telephone conference with your American boss. Explain the problem to him/her and try to negotiate a solution.

Unit 1, Exercise 11 — File 01

Call 1

Your name is Alex Schmidt. You work for NeuBau GmbH as Tanja Steinmann's PA (personal assistant). It's ten o'clock when the phone rings. Answer the phone and help the caller. (Tanja is in a meeting until 12.30, but she is free for the rest of the day.)

Call 2

Your name is Frank/Fran Sharp. You work for Gieser Insurance Ltd. Call Jasta-Karling and ask to speak to the CEO, Karsten Böse. You don't know him, but you want to sell him some insurance. Try as hard as you can to speak to him – don't listen to the secretary's excuses! Important: don't say why you are calling. If you say you want to sell insurance, the secretary won't let you talk to the boss.

Unit 2, Exercise 7 — File 02

First write down the words your partner spells for you (1–4).

1 _____
2 _____
3 _____
4 _____

Did you get it right? Spell the words 1–4 back to your partner to check your spelling.

Finally, spell the place names below (5–8) for your partner. (The words in brackets tell you where you can find these places – they do exist!)

5 Xinjiang Uygur Zizhiqu (China)
6 Vyerkhnyadzvinsk (Belarus)
7 Romorantin-Lanthenay (France)
8 Mariscal Estigarribia (Paraguay)

Unit 2, Exercise 10 — File 03

Call 1

You would like to buy some electronic components. Call RFM Electronics and ask about their prices. (Perhaps they can also send you a price list.) You also have a problem with a component you bought from RFM last month – ask for the telephone number of the customer service department.

TD2002V Audio Amplifier
UGN3505W Magnetic Sensor
6M138 Optocoupler
75AC965 Transceiver

Call 2

You work for NDL Inc. Two days ago you placed an order with BrightFuture Pharmaceuticals. Someone from BrightFuture will call and ask about an address. Your business address is:

1207 Huntington Avenue, Suite 142
San Francisco, CA 94090

The address for deliveries is:

1209 Huntington Avenue
San Francisco, CA 94090

Your email address is:
purchasing@ndl-corporation.com
Your cell phone number: +1 (202) 841-4588.

Unit 3, Exercise 4 — File 04

Call 1

Your name is Jens Düring. You are going to phone your client Monica Thompson from Kilfek AG. Unfortunately she is not in the office so you will have to leave a message on her answering machine. Plan what you are going to say, then call her and leave the message. Here is the information you need.

Hi,
I'm afraid there is a problem with the invoice you sent us last week. The total seems to be incorrect. Could you check this and get back to me?

Thanks,
Monica

I checked the invoice – there's a mistake in it. Can you phone her back and tell her we'll send her a new invoice asap? Thanks!
Rachel

PS Don't forget to apologize for our mistake!

Call 2

You are Jens Düring. You will be in and out of the office for the next three days. Prepare a greeting for your voicemail service, saying when you will be available. Read it out to the caller. Then listen and make a note of the caller's message.

Unit 3, Exercise 10   File 05

Call 1

Your name is Gert/Gertrud Jung and you work for Quine and Frege, an architect's office. Your business partner Gina Wilson from Soncha Engineering sent you an email but forgot to include the attachment. It's an important document and you need it by tomorrow. Call Gina and ask her to send you the document again.

Call 2

Your name is Rosanna/Ross Wall and you work for Bernes Insurance. Your colleague Sal Larkin is out of the office at the moment. Someone will call and leave a message for him. Write down the message, checking all the details to make sure you understand them. Make sure you get the person's office phone number and mobile number.

Unit 4, Exercise 13   File 06

Each box represents one hour – the yellow boxes are when you are busy. Write appointments in the yellow boxes. Think of appointments which are realistic for you, for example a meeting with a client, a sales presentation, dinner with a business partner. Then role-play the three telephone conversations with your partner.

	Monday	Tuesday	Wednesday	Thursday	Friday
9 am					
10 am					
11 am					
12 noon					
1 pm					
2 pm					
3 pm					
4 pm					

Call 1

Your partner wants to meet you next week. (S)He will call you to arrange a time to meet. (Remember that you are busy at the times marked by the yellow boxes.)

Call 2

Something has come up and you need to change the time of the appointment with your partner. Call him/her, explain why you need to change the appointment and find a new time.

Call 3

Your partner will call you about the meeting. (S)He is talking on a mobile phone and the connection is not very good. You will need to ask him/her to repeat some things.

Unit 5, Exercise 10   File 07

Call 1

You work for a car rental company called Easy Auto. A customer will call you to make a complaint. Deal with the complaint as politely and efficiently as you can. Note: you were on holiday last week, so any mistakes made then were not your fault!

Call 2

You work for Klupp, a German engineering company. TransFast, a British translation agency, recently translated your website into English. However your boss has found some mistakes in the translation. Call TransFast and complain.

Here are some of the mistakes I've found on the website:
- *'Kühlrohr' is 'cooling pipe', not 'cool tube'*
- *'Stahlseil' is 'steel cable', not 'steel rope'*
- *'Beton' is 'concrete', not 'cement'(!)*

There were other mistakes too, but these are enough to use as examples. Can you call them and tell them about the mistakes? Make sure you find out what they'll do to solve the problem. Thanks!

Unit 6, Exercise 10   File 08

You work for Gilee and Soare, an American multi-national accounting firm. It is time for your weekly telephone conversation with your German subsidiary. Your contact person (who reports directly to you) is currently head of a three-person team which is doing an audit on a large German company. The project is already over budget. Ask for a status report on the project, and find out what your contact person is going to do to solve the problems on the project.

Answer key

page 5

1

	Call 1	Call 2	Call 3
Who is calling?	John Ellis	Karen Miller	Bob
Who does he/she want to speak to?	Jörg Seide	Maria	Jörg Seide
Does he/she get through?	No. Jörg is in a meeting.	No. Maria's line is engaged.	Yes. But he is on the other line.
If not, why not?			
What will happen next?	Jörg will call back.	Karen will try again.	Jörg will call Bob back.

page 6

2
1 speaking
2 tell, called
3 here
4 wanted
5 hang, connection
6 afraid, engaged
7 calling
8 get
9 hear
10 line

a 1,3 b 9 c 4 d 5 e 6,10 f 7 g 2,8

3   **Answer**
1 Could I speak to Jörg Seide, please?   a, c, h
2 Can I take a message?   f, j
3 Could you ask him to call me back?   a, c
4 Could you tell me your name again?   d
5 Does Mr Seide have your number?   b
6 Is she there at the moment?   g
7 Shall I put you through to her?   f, j
8 Can I just ask what it's about?   i
9 Can I call you back in ten minutes?   a, c
10 Have you got my mobile number?   e

page 7

4   **more formal**
Could you please hold?
Can I just ask what it's about?
Thank you.
Certainly.
Shall I put you through to her?

less formal
Hang on a moment.
What's it about?
Thanks.
Sure.
Do you want to speak to her?

5 1 b 2 c 3 (not used on the telephone) 4 a

6 In call 1, Sylvia says Mr Ellis because the caller has a higher status than her, and also because she doesn't know him. However he calls her Sylvia because she has a lower status than him.
In call 2, Sylvia and Karen know each other (even if only from speaking on the phone) and so they use first names with each other, although Karen probably has a higher status than Sylvia.
In call 3, Jürgen and Bob use first names with each other because they know each other. It's also a sign of a close working relationship.

page 8

7 (model answers)
2 No, I'm actually from Austria.
3 I'm afraid he's not here.
4 Actually, I'll call back later.

5 I'm afraid I won't be in the office tomorrow. / Actually, I won't be in the office tomorrow.
6 I'm afraid Heather's line is engaged. / Heather's line is actually engaged.

8 (model answers)
2 I'm afraid she's having lunch at the moment.
3 I'm sorry, but she's actually on another line.
4 I'm afraid she's out of the office today.
5 I'm afraid she's not available at the moment.
6 I'm sorry, but she's in a meeting at the moment.

page 9

9 (model answer)
A Kroste International. Raymond Pitt speaking.
B Hi Raymond. It's Patrick here. How are you? Did you have a good holiday in New York?
A It was really great, thanks. But I feel I need another holiday to recover!
B I can imagine. Listen Raymond, I actually wanted to talk to Lorraine. Is she there at the moment?
A I'm afraid she's not. She had to leave early today. Would you like to leave a message for her?
B Yes please. Could you ask her to call me back tomorrow morning?
A I'll do that. Well, thanks for calling Patrick. Bye now.

10 a 3 b 1 c 2 d 8 e 4 f 7 g 5 h 6

1 catch
2 could
3 up
4 wrong
5 line
6 cut
7 spell
8 slowly

page 10

12 across
1 CALL BACK
4 EXTENSION
5 MOBILE
7 PUT THROUGH
10 AFRAID
11 ENGAGED

down
1 CONNECTION
2 CALLING
3 MESSAGE
6 SPEAKING
8 HOLD
9 CATCH

The mystery word is TELEPHONE.

page 11

13 (suggested answers)
1 Elke Heide speaking.
2 This is Jan Müller. Can I speak to Ms (or Mrs) Sanders, please?
3 I'll call back later.
4 Brenda isn't in the office / is out of the office today.
5 Do you have my mobile (or cell phone) number?
6 I'm afraid Mr Schmidt isn't in the office today.
7 I'll tell him that you called.

page 12

Picking up
1 a six hundred and forty-seven
b nine thousand two hundred and thirty-five
c one million, five hundred and seventy-four thousand, three hundred and eighty-nine

d   one point nine five five
e   fifteen euros (and) forty (cents)
f   oh oh (or: zero zero) four nine, three oh (or: zero), two
    nine seven oh (or: zero), double six (or: six six) three four

2 A comma shows the thousand position in a number.
   A point shows the decimal place.

3 a   underscore
   b   at
   c   hyphen (or: dash)
   d   dot
   e   (forward) slash
   f   back slash
   g   hash sign / pound sign (chiefly AE) / number
      (The first two terms are frequently used for pre-paid
      phone cards and multi-choice automated phone
      services.)
   h   asterisk
   i   open bracket
   j   close bracket

1 *relay switch*
   model RS 786 877

   unit price:
   1000 units+ €1.65 1.56
   2000 units+ € 11.39 1.49

   Misha Oberemok
   delivery address

   Mitseevitch Ulittsa 6 Mitskevich
   97000 Kiev 79000 Ulitsa
   Fax no. (+380 44)
      244 4240 42 04

page 13

2 Call 1 1 about   3 was   5 right
        2 right   4 tell   6 catch

   Call 2 1 calling 3 pen   5 read
        2 check 4 spell 6 again

3 (model answers)
   2 Could you tell me your name?
   3 I just wanted to check the address.
   4 What was your name again?
   5 What did you want to know?
   6 Could you tell me what your charge for delivery would
      be?
   7 Could you tell me how long it would take to send it?
   8 I just wanted to ask if you have time to meet
      tomorrow.

page 14

4 1 To Germany?   4 Let me just read that back to you.
   2 Did you say   5 And your name was
   3 Sorry, was that 6 So that's

page 15

5 (model answers)
   2 Sorry, did you say *98* King Street?
   3 Let me just read that back to you. Your number is 091
      210 3885.
   4 Thursday, right.
   5 Prentice, right.
   6 Sorry, did you say €72.90 or €72.19?

6

1	2	3	4	5	6	7
A	B	F	I	O	Q	R
H	C	L	Y		U	
J	D	M			W	
K	E	N				
	G	S				
	P	X				
	T	Z (BE)				
	V					
	Z (AE)					

page 16

8 3 Kevin dot Stevens at A F G hyphen* consulting dot C A
   4 Margaret underscore Peterson at zebra dot I T
   5 w w w dot rent hyphen* a hyphen* car dot com
      (* dash also possible)

9 1 Do you have a pen?   H
   2 Let me just read that back to you.   F (J)
   3 I'm calling about the order you faxed us yesterday. A
   4 Are you the right person to ask?   B
   5 What would you like to know?   C (G)
   6 Let me just check that.   J (F)
   7 Would you like me to spell that for you?   I
   8 What was your question?   G (C)
   9 Can I check that and get back to you?   D
   10 Can you just give me your phone number?   E

page 17

11 (model answers)
   1 Do you have a pen?
   2 The order number is A for apple, E for elephant,
      V for Venice, zero two six.
   3 Was that D for David or B for Bob?
   4 His email address is Tom hyphen (or: dash) Baker at
      Martins dot D E.
   5 Sorry, I didn't catch that. Did you say thirteen or
      thirty?

UNIT 3

page 19

1 (model answers)
   For Heike Lorenz / From Walter Jackson
   Please call and confirm date and time for project
   meeting.
   The 10th is OK for him. Tel: 032 345 8395

   For Jürgen Petersen / From Seth Prescott
   He's doing a sales presentation for a prospective client
   and wants to meet with you on Friday at 9 or 10 am for 2
   hours to talk about the 'technical stuff'. He didn't leave a
   number.

   The second message is confusing because it is poorly
   structured, Seth contradicts himself, he hasn't checked
   his facts, and he takes too long to give the message.

page 20

2 1 reached   5 beep   9 confirmed
   2 Unfortunately 6 This   10 again
   3 available 7 calling 11 case
   4 leave   8 get   12 soon

3 (model answers)
Hi. This is Heike Lorenz calling for Walter Jackson. Walter, I just wanted to confirm that the project meeting will take place on the 10th, starting at 9 am. I'm looking forward to seeing you then. Bye now.

Hello. This is Seth Prescott calling for Jürgen Petersen. I have a sales presentation for a prospective client, and I wanted to ask you if we could meet next Friday to talk about the technical aspects. We'll need about two hours so maybe we can meet at 9 am? Could you please call me back today to let me know if you can do it? My number is 9083 5209. Thanks a lot. Bye.

page 21

5 a call 2   b call 1   c call 2   d call 2   e call 1

(messages – model answers)
Jonathon, Ricardo Fonseca from Aresto called about the EuroMedical fair next week. He wanted to know if you're going and if you and he can meet. Please call him back. He'll be in the office until 5 pm today.

Elaine Sloan called about the team for the new marketing campaign. She wanted to know if Henry can still be on the team if they shift the deadline back a week. Call back today on 44 141 223 4569.

6 1 I'm afraid Jonathan isn't here at the moment.
2 Would you like to leave a message for him?
3 Let me get a pen.
4 Shall I ask Jonathan to call you back?
5 Does he have your number?
6 I'll make sure Jonathan gets your message.

a ... the email you sent me yesterday.
b ... Henry was too busy to join the team.
c ... that we could take Maria instead.
d ... as soon as I've had the chance to speak to him?
e ... just in case?
f ... call you straight back.

page 22

7 (model answers)
2 She told me that maybe we could find another supplier.
3 He said it would be difficult to schedule a new meeting.
4 They asked if we could deliver earlier.
5 You mentioned that you had hired two new employees.
6 He told me that he was going to the UK in June.

8 1 at
2 after, on (or AE: at)
3 for
4 about
5 to
6 in, until

page 23

9 b Can you please give me your number again just in case? — 5
c Could you get back to me on this asap, please? — 8
d Would you like to leave a message for her? — 3
e I'm afraid she isn't here at the moment. — 6
f I'm calling about the email you sent me yesterday. — 7
g I'll make sure she gets your message. — 4
h I think you have my number already. — 2

page 25

11 1 You can reach me on (not 'under') 544 332 64.
2 Would you like to leave a message for her?
3 Eileen asked me to call her back.
4 This is Mary Lamb. I'm calling about the meeting.
5 He told (not 'said') me that he had already sent the letter.

UNIT 4

page 26

Picking up
1 b, c, and e are not possible.
2 a half (past) six
b just before/after
c quarter to/past
d midnight
e midday/noon
3 a January 2, 2006
b 1 February 2006
4 b, d, and e are not possible.

1 Simon makes an appointment with Alexa to meet at 10 am on Wednesday in his office.

page 27

2 Suggesting a meeting or an appointment
(* phrases from part 2)
Could we schedule a meeting for next month?*
Do you have time to meet tomorrow?*

Asking about or suggesting a time to meet
When would suit you?
Would that be OK for you?
We could meet in the evening ...
Well, how about Wednesday morning?
Shall we say 10 o'clock in my office?
What about Thursday?*
Where would be the best place to meet?*

Saying if a time is convenient or not
I think that should be possible.
I should be free on Tuesday morning, though.
Tuesday's bad for me, I'm afraid.
I'm tied up all day.
Sorry, I'm booked up that evening too.
Yes, that would be good for me.
Yes, I'm free then.*

Confirming an arrangement
I'll see you on Wednesday, then.
OK, so that's 2 pm in the conference room.*

3 (model answer)
A Gina Kilshaw.
B Hi Gina. It's René here. I was wondering if you might have time to meet tomorrow, maybe at 10 am?
A Sorry, I'm tied up all morning. What about in the afternoon?
B Sorry, I'm booked up in the afternoon. How about Friday at 10?
A Yes, that would be good for me. Shall we meet in my office?
B Sounds good. So that's Friday at 10 am in your office.
A Great. See you then.

page 28

4 2 's flying   4 's having   6 's meeting
   3 's meeting   5 's having   7 's coming

page 29

5 3 in   4 on   5 Ø
   6 Ø   7 Ø   8 on
   9 at (BE) / on (AE)   10 at (BE) / on (AE)   11 at
   12 at   13 in   14 in
   15 in

6 1 f   2 c   3 e   4 b   5 a   6 d

page 30

7 (model answer)
   A Hello. Jason Moore speaking.
   B Hi Jason. It's Petra Klein here.
   A Petra! How nice to hear from you. How are things in Cologne?
   B Pretty busy, as usual. How's the weather in England?
   A Terrible! What's it like with you?
   B Not so bad. We had a bit of sun today. So, Jason, I actually wanted to ask you about the figures you sent me …

8 The following sentences are in the dialogue: 1, 4, 5, 8

(model answer)
Simon – Alexa Johnston called. She asked if she could change the time of her meeting with you tomorrow. I changed it to 9 o'clock. Hope that's okay.

page 31

9 1 wondering, changed   4 bit, postponed
   2 wanted, missed   5 possible, delayed
   3 possibly, lasted

10 She's still waiting for the train and wants to tell Simon that she might be a few minutes late.

   1 waiting   4 catch   7 delays
   2 might   5 see   8 losing
   3 breaking   6 latest   9 better

11 1 c, d, h   2 d, e, g   3 d, e, g   4 a   5 b, f   6 f

page 32

12 1 date   4 bring forward   7 postpone
   2 cancel   5 arrangements   8 arrange
   3 appointment   6 date

14 (model answers)
   1 I'm afraid something has come up.
   2 She has an appointment (not 'date'!) with the MD.
   3 I might be a few minutes late (not 'too late'!).
   4 I'm flying to New York on Saturday.
   5 I'm tied up all day.
   6 I should be free on Wednesday afternoon.

UNIT 5

page 34

1 a 2   b 4   c 1   d 3
   A 1   B 2   C 4   D 3   E 2   F 4   G 1   H 3

page 35

2 There's a problem with the latest consignment: some of the boxes contain the wrong sensor model (the FR 388 instead of the FR 346). To solve the problem, Reva will send Abby 130 units of the FR 346 by express delivery with Swift Logistics.

   1 consignment   4 FR 346   7 Swift
   2 boxes   5 FR 388   8 pick
   3 sensor   6 express

3 1 appears   4 get   7 mix-up
   2 sorry   5 this   8 personally
   3 exactly   6 sorting

   describe a problem   1
   clarify what the problem is   3
   apologize   2, 7
   say how you will solve the problem   4, 5

page 36

4 (model answers)
   2 Unfortunately you delivered the consignment to the wrong address.
   3 The total on the bill appears to be wrong.
   4 I'm afraid we have a slight problem with the equipment you sold us.
   5 You seem to have sent us the wrong model.
   6 Unfortunately you gave us the incorrect information.

page 37

5 1 There appears to be a mistake
   2 Could you tell me
   3 Please accept my apologies
   4 I'll make sure that gets sorted out
   5 It seems you sent us
   6 I'm really sorry about
   7 sorry again about the mix-up

The first conversation is more formal; the second is more informal.

6 2 'll have   4 'll give
   3 'll personally make sure   5 'll deliver

page 38

7 (model answer)
   A I'm afraid there seems to be a small problem with your delivery dates.
   B Oh dear. Can you explain what the problem is exactly?
   A Well, in our discussions you said you could deliver by the end of September. But in the contract you sent me, it says delivery will be in the middle of October.
   B Sorry, that's entirely my fault. I forgot we had agreed on September. I'll change the contract and send you the new version.
   A Thanks.
   B No problem. And sorry again for that mistake. Bye now.

8 1 Michel
2 Euromarché
3 Receipts come out blank when printed
4 New ink cartridge sent to customer

9 1 right   3 details   5 questions, call
2 detail   4 case   6 any

page 39

11 (model answers)
1 There appears/seems to be a small problem with the invoice.
2 That must be really annoying.
3 You should have the consignment first thing tomorrow.
4 Thanks for sorting that out.
5 I'll (personally) make sure it doesn't happen again.

UNIT 6

page 40

1 1 A & M   5 five
2 processor   6 ten
3 middle   7 quotation
4 shift work

page 41

2 1 d 2 a 3 f 4 b 5 c 6 e

3 4 would cost   8 would be
5 would/could cause   9 asked
6 reduced   11 could rent
7 would/could cause   12 could work

page 42

4 (model answers)
2 We might be able to deliver by the end of the week.
3 I would say that we can solve the problem.
4 It will probably be difficult.
5 (I think) I can provisionally say that we can change the specifications of the product.

5 1 Davis   4 discount
2 price   5 five per cent
3 ten per cent   6 500

page 43

6 1 follow up   4 may be true
2 didn't you   5 something
3 interrupt

7 (model answer)
A Sandra Caspers.
B Hi Sandra. It's Rainer Thide here.
A Oh, hi Rainer. What can I do for you?
B I'm calling about the prices you quoted us for software development costs. They seem a bit too high for me. Is there any possibility you can lower the price?
A Well, we could reduce the price a little if you changed your operating system to Linux. You know how it's free and it's also cheaper to …

B Sorry, can I interrupt you there? All our computers run on Windows, and there's no possibility of changing at the moment. But what about if you simplified the specification? I mean, there seems to be …
A Can I just say something? The specification we gave you is the absolute minimum. We can't simplify it. But we might be able to outsource some of the work to our partners in India. That would be cheaper.
B That sounds like it might work. Yes, maybe we can do that.

page 44

8 1 g   5 i   9 d
2 h   6 j   10 c
3 b   7 e
4 f   8 a

9 1 follow up our conversation
2 tight schedule
3 meet the deadline
4 That depends
5 time frame
6 That's difficult to say
7 ballpark figure
8 off the top of my head
9 prepare a quotation
10 room to manoeuvre

page 45

11 (model answers)
1 I would be pleased if we could work with you.
2 That sounds reasonable.
3 I don't know off the top of my head.
4 Can I interrupt you there for a second?
5 Can we meet the deadline? – That depends.

page 46

Across		Down	
7	just in case	1	ballpark figure
8	up	2	happen
10	spell	3	actually
13	sound	4	bring forward
14	calling	5	suit
15	make sure	9	message
19	answering machine	10	should
23	mentioned	11	extension
28	else	12	wanted
29	about	16	appreciate
31	back	17	appears
32	urgently	18	diary
33	engaged	20	wrong
34	catch	21	complain
		22	until
		24	delighted
		25	interrupt
		26	through
		27	straight
		28	exactly
		30	up

Transcripts

UNIT 1, EXERCISE 1

Call 1

Sylvia	Micah Information Systems. Sylvia speaking.
John	Hello. This is John Ellis from Retex Plc. Could I speak to Jörg Seide, please?
Sylvia	I'm afraid Mr Seide is in a meeting. Can I take a message?
John	Yes, please. Could you ask him to call me back?
Sylvia	Certainly. Could you tell me your name again, please?
John	My name is John Ellis. And I'm calling from Retex Plc.
Sylvia	Does Mr Seide have your number?
John	Actually, I don't think he does. It's 00 44 140 397 834.
Sylvia	397 834. That's great. Okay, Mr Ellis, I'll tell Mr Seide you called.
John	Thanks very much, Sylvia.
Sylvia	You're welcome. Bye now.
John	Bye.

Call 2

Sylvia	Micah Information Systems. Sylvia speaking.
Karen	Hi Sylvia. It's Karen Miller here.
Sylvia	Oh, hi Karen. How are you?
Karen	Fine, thanks. And you?
Sylvia	Not so bad. A bit busy, as always.
Karen	I can imagine. Listen Sylvia, I actually wanted to speak to Maria. Is she there at the moment?
Sylvia	Yes, she is. Shall I put you through to her?
Karen	That would be great.
Sylvia	Can I just ask what it's about?
Karen	I wanted to ask her about the project meeting next week.
Sylvia	Thanks, Karen. Just hang on a moment while I make the connection. … Sorry, Karen. I'm afraid Maria's line is engaged.
Karen	Oh, that's a pity. I'll try calling later.
Sylvia	Shall I give you her extension number?
Karen	Yes, please. Let me just get a pen. Okay.
Sylvia	It's 113.
Karen	113. Right. Thanks, Sylvia. Bye now.
Sylvia	Bye.

Call 3

Jörg	Seide.
Bob	Hi Jörg. It's Bob here.
Jörg	Oh, hi Bob. Nice to hear from you. How's business?
Bob	Oh, can't complain. How are things with you?
Jörg	Fine, thanks. Listen Bob, can I call you back in ten minutes? I'm actually talking to someone on the other line.
Bob	Sure, no problem. Have you got my mobile number?
Jörg	Yes, I have.
Bob	Great. Speak to you then.
Jörg	Bye.

UNIT 1, EXERCISE 10

Call 1

A	So, we have a meeting planned for next Monday.
B	Sorry, I didn't catch that.
A	I said, we have a meeting planned for next Monday.
B	Ah, okay.

Call 2

A	The serial number is KLT/9090/34.
B	Sorry, could you repeat that please?
A	Sorry, I said the serial number is KLT/9090/34.

Call 3

A	Yes, well, I think there could be a problem with the project schedule.
B	Sorry, can you speak up a bit, please?
A	Sorry. I said, I think there could be a problem with the project schedule.

Call 4

A	Petrex Plastics. Simon speaking.
B	Hi. Is Claire Brown there?
A	Sorry, I think you have the wrong number. There's no one of that name here.
B	Oh, sorry about that.
A	No problem.

Call 5

A	Anyway, when I arrived last night, I realized I forgot to take the contract with me.
B	Sorry, this is a really bad line. I didn't catch that.
A	I said, I forgot to take the contract. Can you send it to me by email?

Call 6

A	So, we should really try to find time next week for a meeting. What do you think? … Hello? Are you there? Hmm. Hi, Chris?
B	Yes, I'm here. Sorry, we got cut off. I don't know what happened.
A	That's okay. Anyway, as I was saying …

Call 7

A	And my last name is MacGilchrist.
B	Sorry, could you spell that for me, please?
A	Of course. It's M-A-C-G-I-L-C-H-R-I-S-T.

Call 8

A	Listen, I have a very quick question about the agenda for tomorrow's meeting. Could you tell me if the new marketing strategy is on the agenda?
B	Sorry, could you speak a little bit more slowly, please?
A	Sorry. I wanted to know if the new marketing strategy is on the agenda for tomorrow's meeting.

UNIT 2, EXERCISE 1

Call 1

Arno	HCE Ltd. Arno Maier speaking. How can I help you?
Neil	Hello. I have a question about your relay switches. Are you the right person to ask?
Arno	Yes, I am. What was your question?

Neil	I'm interested in the switch model RS 877, but I couldn't find a price for it on your website. Could you tell me what the unit price would be for orders over a thousand units?
Arno	Hang on a second, let me just check that in our system. That was the RS 877, right?
Neil	Yes, that's right.
Arno	OK … The unit price for a thousand units or more would be 1 euro 56 cents. If you order two thousand units or more, then the unit price drops to … let me see … 1 euro 49 cents.
Neil	Sorry, I didn't catch the second price.
Arno	It's 1 euro 49 cents.
Neil	OK. Right, so that's 1 euro 56 cents for a thousand units or over, and 1 euro 49 cents for two thousand units or over.
Arno	That's right.
Neil	Great. Well, thank you very much.
Arno	You're welcome. Just let me know if there's anything else I can do for you.
Neil	I'll do that. Goodbye.
Arno	Bye.

Call 2

14

Misha	Dorogo Engineering. Misha Oberemok speaking.
Arno	Hi Misha. It's Arno Maier from HCE here.
Misha	Hello Arno. How are you?
Arno	Not bad, thanks. Listen Misha, I'm calling about the order you faxed us yesterday.
Misha	Uh huh.
Arno	The delivery address written on the fax isn't very clear, and I just wanted to check it.
Misha	OK. Let me just find my copy of the order. One second. OK. Do you have a pen?
Arno	Yes I do.
Misha	Right. The address is Mitskevich Ulitsa 6, 79000 Kiev. Would you like me to spell that for you?
Arno	Yes please.
Misha	OK. It's M-I-T-S-K-E-V-I-C-H, new word, U-L-I-T-S-A, number 6.
Arno	Let me just read that back to you. It's M-I-T-S-K-E-V-I-C-H, new word, U-L-I-T-S-A, number 6. Is that right?
Misha	Yes, that's right.
Arno	Sorry, what was the post code again?
Misha	79000.
Arno	79000. OK. And Kiev is spelt K-I-E-V, is that right?
Misha	Exactly.
Arno	OK. And one last thing. We don't have your fax number and the number on your fax was hard to read. What were the last four digits?
Misha	Mmm. That's 42 04.
Arno	Sorry, did you say 42 04 or 42 14?
Misha	42 04.
Arno	Great. OK, Misha, I think that was everything. I'll make sure the order gets sent off today. Thanks very much for your help.
Misha	No problem. Speak to you later.
Arno	Bye.

UNIT 3, EXERCISE 1

Message 1

15

Hello. You've reached Leze Logistics. Unfortunately no one is available to take your call at the moment. Our normal office hours are 9 to 5, Mondays to Fridays. Please leave a message after the beep or send us a fax on 021 991 8814. Thank you.

Hello. This is Walter Jackson calling for Heike Lorenz. Heike, I'm calling about the planned project meeting. You asked me if the 10th would be okay for me, and I just wanted to confirm that it is. Maybe you can get back to me as soon as you've confirmed the date and time with everyone. I think you have my number already, but here it is again, just in case. It's 032 345 8395. Hope to speak to you soon. Bye.

Message 2

16

Hi. Can you help me next, um, what day is the tenth? Thursday? No, Friday. That's right, Friday. Maybe at 10 am? Let me think – would that give us enough time? We could also meet at 9. That might be better actually. Oh, I almost forgot – I need you to talk about technical stuff. We'll probably need two hours. It's for a prospective client – I'm doing a sales presentation for them. Oh, this is Seth Prescott by the way. And this message is for Jürgen … Jürgen … er … Petersen, that's it, Jürgen Petersen. Bye. Oh, wait a moment, I don't think you have my number. It's …

UNIT 3, EXERCISE 5

Call 1

17

Anke	JKL Consulting. Anke Schmidt speaking.
Ricardo	Hello. This is Ricardo Fonseca from Aresto. Could I speak to Jonathan Leary, please?
Anke	Oh, I'm afraid Jonathan isn't here at the moment. Would you like to leave a message for him?
Ricardo	Yes, please.
Anke	Just a moment. Let me get a pen. [pause] Okay, I'm ready now. Go ahead.
Ricardo	Right. I was calling about the EuroMedical trade fair next week. Jonathan mentioned that he was thinking about going. So I just wanted to check if he'll be there, and if so, if he has time to meet me.
Anke	Let me just make sure that I got that right. You're going to the EuroMedical trade fair next week, and you'd like to know if Jonathan will be there, and if the two of you can meet.
Ricardo	That's right.
Anke	Shall I ask Jonathan to call you back?
Ricardo	Yes, that would be good.
Anke	OK. Erm … does he have your number?
Ricardo	Yes, he does. I'll be in the office until about 5 pm today if he wants to call me.
Anke	That's great. I'll make sure Jonathan gets your message.
Ricardo	Thanks very much.
Anke	You're welcome. Bye for now.
Ricardo	Bye.

Call 2
18

Anke	JKL Consulting. Anke Schmidt speaking.
Elaine	Hi Anke. This is Elaine Sloan.
Anke	Oh hi, Elaine. How are you doing?
Elaine	Fine thanks, and you?
Anke	Oh, can't complain. So, what can I do for you?
Elaine	I'm calling about the email you sent me yesterday, about the team for the new marketing campaign. You said that Henry was too busy to join the team and you told me that we could take Maria instead.
Anke	That's right.
Elaine	Well, we would really like to have Henry if possible, so I wanted to make a suggestion. Do you think Henry would have time if we shifted the deadline back, say, a week or so?
Anke	Mmm, that might be possible, but I'll have to talk about it with Henry first.
Elaine	Of course.
Anke	Can I call you back later today as soon as I've had the chance to speak to him?
Elaine	Sure. I'll be here all day. You've got my number, right?
Anke	I think so, but can you give it to me again just in case?
Elaine	Yes. It's 44 for Britain, then 141 223 4569.
Anke	Let me read that back to you. 141 223 4569, is that right?
Elaine	Yes, that's right.
Anke	Great. Okay, I'll talk to Henry and call you straight back.
Elaine	Thanks Anke. Talk to you later.
Anke	Bye.

UNIT 4, EXERCISE 1

19

Simon	Simon Mellor.
Alexa	Hi Simon. It's Alexa Johnston here.
Simon	Oh, hi Alexa. How are you doing?
Alexa	Can't complain. How are things in Frankfurt?
Simon	Oh, you know what it's like. Business as usual! So, what can I do for you, Alexa?
Alexa	Well, I'm going to be in Frankfurt next week, and I was wondering if you might have time to meet me for an hour or two while I'm in town. It would give us the chance to talk about the Allianz project, among other things.
Simon	Yes, that's a good idea. Let me just think for a moment … I think that should be possible. I just need to check my diary. Hang on a sec. (pause) Right. When would suit you?
Alexa	Let me think. I'm flying in on Monday morning. I'll be in a meeting all afternoon and then I'm having dinner with my client in the evening. I should be free on Tuesday morning, though. Would that be OK for you?
Simon	Tuesday's bad for me, I'm afraid. I'm tied up all day. We could meet in the evening for something to eat, though.
Alexa	Sorry, I'm booked up that evening too. Mmm, this is getting a bit difficult.
Simon	Well, how about Wednesday morning?
Alexa	Yes, that would be good for me.
Simon	Brilliant. Shall we say 10 o'clock in my office?

Alexa	Yes, that sounds good. Oh, by the way, I'll have my mobile with me if you need to get in touch. You have the number, right?
Simon	Yes, I do. OK, Alexa, I'll see you on Wednesday, then.
Alexa	Excellent. See you.
Simon	Bye.

UNIT 4, EXERCISE 4

20

Hilary	JPL Consulting. Hilary Wilkins speaking.
Anna	Hello Hilary. This is Anna Roth from Frankfurt. Is Alexa there?
Hilary	I'm afraid she isn't. Can I help at all?
Anna	Well, a colleague told me that Alexa is coming to Frankfurt next week. I'd like to see her while she's here, if she has time.
Hilary	Okay. Well, let me look at her schedule and we'll figure something out. When would suit you best?
Anna	I'm pretty flexible. Maybe you can tell me when she's free?
Hilary	Let me see. Okay, so she's flying to Frankfurt first thing on Monday morning. Then she's meeting a client at 12. In the evening she's having dinner with a friend.
Anna	Hmm. Sounds like she's quite busy. What about Tuesday?
Hilary	Well, she's free on Tuesday morning. But then she's having lunch with a colleague at 1 and she's meeting someone in the evening.
Anna	Okay. And Wednesday?
Hilary	That's pretty full. She has a couple of meetings during the day then she's coming back to London in the evening.
Anna	Okay. Well, maybe you can pencil me in on Tuesday morning. Say, 10 o'clock?
Hilary	10 o'clock on Tuesday. Okay, I'll double-check that with Alexa and send you a quick email to confirm the meeting.
Anna	Wonderful. Thanks for your help.
Hilary	You're welcome. Bye now.

UNIT 4, EXERCISE 8

21

Thorsten	Thorsten Hofmeister.
Alexa	Hello, this is Alexa Johnston. May I speak to Simon Mellor, please?
Thorsten	He's actually in a meeting at the moment. But maybe I can help you.
Alexa	Well, I'm calling about our meeting tomorrow. I'm afraid something has come up. One of my clients has brought forward our appointment in the afternoon to 12 o'clock. So I wanted to ask Simon if we could meet a bit earlier in the morning, so that I don't have to rush.
Thorsten	Let me just check Simon's schedule. OK … How about 9 o'clock?
Alexa	Yes, that sounds fine.
Thorsten	Great. I'll tell Simon about the new time. And just give me a call if there are any more changes.
Alexa	I'll do that. Thanks very much for your help.
Thorsten	You're welcome. Bye now.

UNIT 4, EXERCISE 10

🔘
22

Simon	Simon Mellor.
Alexa	Hi Simon, Alexa again.
Simon	Oh, hi Alexa. What's up?
Alexa	I'm actually still waiting for the train so I'm afraid I might be a few minutes late.
Simon	Sorry, you're breaking up a little. I didn't catch that last part.
Alexa	I said I might be a few minutes late to your office.
Simon	Oh, OK. That's no problem. I'll see you when I see you.
Alexa	I should be there by 9.15 at the latest, but I'll call you again if there are any more delays. Listen, I think I'm losing the connection. I'd better go.
Simon	Sure. See you in a few minutes.
Alexa	Bye.

UNIT 5, EXERCISE 1

🔘
23

Extract 1

A	I'm calling from RS Plastics. There appears to be a mistake on the invoice you sent us.
B	I'm very sorry about that. Let me put you through to our accounts department. They'll sort it out for you.
A	Thanks.

🔘
24

Extract 2

A	Anyway, I'm actually calling about the email you sent me. You seem to have forgotten the attachment.
B	Oh dear. Sorry about that. I'll send you the file right away.
A	That would be great, thanks.

🔘
25

Extract 3

A	It's about the delivery we received yesterday. Some of the components don't seem to work.
B	Really? I'm very sorry about that. Can I check that and call you back?
A	Sure, no problem.

🔘
26

Extract 4

A	There's a problem with our network. The email server doesn't seem to be working.
B	You actually need to speak to our technical support hotline. Unfortunately I can't put you through directly, but let me give you the number.
B	That would be good, thanks.

UNIT 5, EXERCISE 2

🔘
27

Reva	Hume Sensors. Reva Burgos speaking.
Abby	Hello Reva, this is Abby Dickson from Sykes Electronics here.
Reva	Oh hello, Abby, how are you?
Abby	I'm a bit stressed to tell the truth. There appears to be a small problem with your latest consignment.
Reva	Oh dear. I'm sorry to hear that. What's the problem exactly?
Abby	Well, you know we ordered your FR 346 sensor last week.
Reva	Yes. 1200 units, if I remember correctly.
Abby	Exactly. Anyway, some of the boxes contain the wrong sensor model, namely the FR 388.
Reva	Oh, I'm very sorry about that. That must be really annoying.

Abby	Well, it has caused problems with our production schedule, to be honest.
Reva	Yes, I can imagine. It's good that you've brought it to my attention. Listen Abby, I'll get on to this problem immediately. How many units are missing exactly?
Abby	Let me just check … 130.
Reva	130. Right. Well, this is what I'm going to do. I'll send you 130 units of the FR 346 by express delivery with Swift Logistics. You should have them first thing tomorrow morning.
Abby	That's excellent. Shall I send you the wrong sensors back?
Reva	Yes, I'll tell the logistics company to pick the boxes up when they deliver the correct units.
Abby	Great. Well, thanks for sorting that out, Reva.
Reva	It's the least I can do. Again, I'm really sorry about the mix-up. I'll personally make sure it doesn't happen again.
Abby	That's great, Reva. Thank you. Talk to you later.
Reva	Bye for now.

UNIT 5, EXERCISE 8

🔘
28

Anja	Nexus Retail Systems. Technical Support Hotline. Anja speaking.
Michel	Hello. This is Michel from Euromarché. There appears to be a problem with our cash register system. Are you the right person to talk to?
Anja	I certainly am. Could you explain the problem in more detail?
Michel	Well, when we want to print receipts they come out blank.
Anja	I see. OK, I'm going to need some more details to solve the problem. First of all, when did this problem start?
Michel	Yesterday afternoon, I think.
Anja	Uh huh. And did the receipts suddenly go blank, or did it happen gradually?
Michel	It happened gradually. First the writing got lighter, and then it disappeared completely.
Anja	In that case, it must be the ink cartridge. The ink must be finished. That's easy to fix. OK, Michel, this is what I'll do. I'll send you a new ink cartridge today. You'll have it by tomorrow.
Michel	And can I install it myself?
Anja	Yes, it's very easy. The instructions are on the packaging, but if you have any questions just give me a call. My name's Anja Schneider, but you can speak to any of our operatives here on the hotline.
Michel	That's great. I'm glad it's nothing serious. Thanks for your help.
Anja	You're very welcome.
Michel	Bye now.
Anja	Bye.

UNIT 6, EXERCISE 1

29

Helen	A & M Semiconductors. Helen Tanner speaking.
Wolfgang	Hello. This is Wolfgang Zimmer calling from K Systems in Cologne.
Helen	Hello Mr Zimmer. What can I do for you?
Wolfgang	We're thinking about placing an order with you for processor chips.
Helen	Really? I'm pleased to hear that.
Wolfgang	The only thing is, we need the chips very urgently. We've just won a contract with a major new customer.
Helen	Congratulations. How quickly do you need the chips exactly?
Wolfgang	We need them by the middle of next month at the latest.
Helen	Right, so that would be in five weeks' time. I have to say that's a pretty tight schedule.
Wolfgang	You're right, but we really need them by then if we're going to meet our project deadlines with our customer. If you weren't able to deliver by then, we would have to go to another supplier. You're our first choice however, so it would be good if we could find a way to work with you.
Helen	Of course I would like that as well. Let me think for a moment. Normally we need six to eight weeks from order to delivery. However, if we introduced shift work at the factory, then we would probably be able to manufacture the chips faster.
Wolfgang	Well, that sounds like it would be feasible.
Helen	Yes, but shift work is more expensive. Would you be prepared to pay more for the chips in order to get them faster?
Wolfgang	That depends. How much more expensive would they be?
Helen	That's difficult to say. I'd need to do the calculations.
Wolfgang	Well, can you give me a ballpark figure?
Helen	Let me think. Off the top of my head, I would say between 5 to 10 per cent more expensive.
Wolfgang	OK. Well, I'll have to check that with my boss, but I think I can provisionally say that we could work with that.
Helen	Great. So maybe you can talk to your boss and I can work out a quotation for you, and then we can talk again.
Wolfgang	Sounds good. How quickly can you prepare the quotation?
Helen	I'll have it ready by tomorrow. I'll send it to you by email, and then we can talk again.
Wolfgang	Great. Talk to you tomorrow, then.
Helen	Bye.

UNIT 6, EXERCISE 5

30

Francesca	Hineman Pharmaceuticals. Francesca Davis speaking.
Viktor	Hello. This is Viktor Klein calling from Swiss Optik in Basel.
Francesca	Ah, Mr Klein, nice to hear from you again.
Viktor	I'm calling because I wanted to follow up our conversation from yesterday. Remember, we talked about a possible order for saline solution.
Francesca	That's right. You said you wanted to compare products and prices from different suppliers, didn't you?
Viktor	Yes. Well I've done that now, and I'm pleased to say that we are interested in your product.
Francesca	Wonderful. Shall I fax you the order form? We could …
Viktor	Sorry, can I interrupt you there? There's actually one small problem. The price you offered us is roughly ten per cent higher than the competition, and I …
Francesca	Well yes, that may be true, but I think you'll find our quality is higher and …
Viktor	Yes, yes, but can I just say something? I wanted to ask if there was any possibility of a discount, say if we ordered a certain quantity. What do you think?
Francesca	Well, I think we have a certain amount of room to manoeuvre, but I would have to check with my boss first. Can I talk to her and get back to you?
Viktor	Certainly.
Francesca	I can do that right now if you don't mind waiting for a couple of minutes. Is that OK?
Viktor	No problem.
Francesca	Great. I'll just put you on hold. … Hello? Mr Klein?
Viktor	Yes, I'm here.
Francesca	Right, I've spoken to my boss and I can offer you a five per cent discount on orders over 500 cases. How does that sound?
Viktor	Five per cent when we order more than 500 cases? That sounds very reasonable. Of course, I'd need to discuss that again with my boss, but I think I can tentatively say that you can expect an order from us in the next couple of days.
Francesca	I'm delighted to hear that. Just let me know if there's anything else I can help you with.
Viktor	I'll do that. Anyway, I'm sure we'll talk soon.
Francesca	I'll look forward to that.
Viktor	Bye now.
Francesca	Bye.

A–Z word list

A

to **accept** [ək'sept] — über-, annehmen
according to [ə'kɔ:dɪŋ tə] — entsprechend
action, to take ~ [teɪk 'ækʃn] — Schritte unternehmen
actually ['æktʃuəli] — eigentlich, wirklich, tatsächlich
advice [əd'vaɪs] — Rat
agency ['eɪdʒənsi] — Agentur, Büro
agenda [ə'dʒendə] — Tagesordnung
aggressive [ə'gresɪv] — aggressiv
to **agree with** [ə'gri: wɪð] — zustimmen
agreement [ə'gri:mənt] — Vertrag, Vereinbarung
air freight ['eə freɪt] — Luftfracht
to **allow** [ə'laʊ] — zulassen
annoying [ə'nɔɪɪŋ] — ärgerlich, lästig
answering machine ['ɑ:nsərɪŋ məʃi:n] — Anrufbeantworter
answerphone (BE) ['ɑ:nsəfəʊn] — Anrufbeantworter
to **apologize** [ə'pɒlədʒaɪz] — sich entschuldigen
apparently [ə'pærəntli] — offensichtlich, anscheinend
appointment [ə'pɔɪntmənt] — Termin, Verabredung
to **appreciate** [ə'pri:ʃɪeɪt] — dankbar sein
to **arrange** [ə'reɪndʒ] — arrangieren, vereinbaren
arrangement [ə'reɪndʒmənt] — Vereinbarung, Termin
asap (as soon as possible) [eɪ es eɪ 'pi:] — so bald/schnell wie möglich
attitude ['ætɪtju:d] — Einstellung, Haltung
audit ['ɔ:dɪt] — Betriebs-, Buchprüfung
available [ə'veɪləbl] — zu sprechen, anwesend

B

ballpark figure [,bɔ:lpɑ:k 'fɪgə] — grobe Abschätzung
battery (rechargeable) ['bætri ,ri:'tʃɑ:dʒəbl] — Akku
beep, after the ~ [,ɑ:ftə ðə 'bi:p] — nach dem Pfeifton
bill [bɪl] — Rechnung
blank [blæŋk] — unbedruckt, leer
body language ['bɒdi læŋgwɪdʒ] — Körpersprache
boss [bɒs] — Chef/in
to **break up** [,breɪk 'ʌp] — zusammenbrechen
to **bring forward** [,brɪŋ 'fɔ:wəd] — vorverlegen
to **bring sth to sb's attention** [,brɪŋ tu ə'tenʃn] — jdn auf etw aufmerksam machen
business card ['bɪznəs kɑ:d] — (Visiten-)Karte
business contact ['bɪznəs kɒntækt] — Geschäftsverbindung
business trip ['bɪznəs trɪp] — Geschäftsreise
busy (AE) ['bɪzi] — besetzt
by the way [baɪ ðə 'weɪ] — übrigens

C

call, to give sb a ~ [gɪv ə 'kɔ:l] — jdn anrufen
to **call again later** [kɔ:l ə,gen 'leɪtə] — später noch einmal anrufen
to **call back** [,kɔ:l 'bæk] — zurückrufen
caller ['kɔ:lə] — Anrufer/in
to **calm down** [,kɑ:m 'daʊn] — beruhigen
campaign [kæm'peɪn] — Kampagne, Aktion
can't complain [kɑ:nt kəm'pleɪn] — (ich) kann nicht klagen
to **cancel** ['kænsl] — absagen
carefully ['keəfəli] — sorgfältig
case [keɪs] — hier: Kiste
cash register ['kæʃ redʒɪstə] — Kasse
to **catch** [kætʃ] — verstehen
cell phone (AE) ['sel fəʊn] — Mobiltelefon, Handy
CEO [,si: i: 'əʊ] — Hauptgeschäftsführer/in
certainly ['sɜ:tnli] — sicherlich, gewiss
challenge ['tʃælɪndʒ] — Herausforderung
challenging ['tʃælɪndʒɪŋ] — eine Herausforderung darstellend
chance, to have the ~ [həv ðə 'tʃɑ:ns] — Gelegenheit haben
charge [tʃɑ:dʒ] — Gebühr

to **chat** ['tʃæt] — plaudern
clarification [,klærəfɪ'keɪʃn] — Klärung
client ['klaɪənt] — Kunde/Kundin
to **come up** [,kʌm 'ʌp] — sich ereignen, sich ergeben
common ['kɒmən] — üblich
communication [kə,mju:nɪ'keɪʃn] — Verständigung, Kommunikation
company culture [,kʌmpəni 'kʌltʃə] — Unternehmenskultur
to **compare** [kəm'peə] — vergleichen
compensation [,kɒmpen'seɪʃn] — Ersatz
competition [,kɒmpə'tɪʃn] — Konkurrenz
to **complain** [kəm'pleɪn] — (sich) beschweren, reklamieren
complaint [kəm'pleɪnt] — Beschwerde, Reklamation
component [kəm'pəʊnənt] — (Einzel-)Teil, Bauteil
confident ['kɒnfɪdənt] — selbstsicher
to **confirm** [kən'fɜ:m] — bestätigen
connection, to lose the ~ [lu:z ðə kə'nekʃn] — die Verbindung verlieren
connection, to make a ~ [meɪk ə kə'nekʃn] — eine Verbindung herstellen
considerate [kən'sɪdərət] — rücksichtsvoll
consignment [kən'saɪnmənt] — (Waren-)Sendung, Lieferung
constantly ['kɒnstəntli] — ständig
contact details ['kɒntækt di:teɪlz] — Kontaktdaten
contact, to have ~ [həv 'kɒntækt] — Kontakt haben
context ['kɒntekst] — Kontext, Zusammenhang
continually [kən'tɪnjuəli] — ständig
contract ['kɒntrækt] — Vertrag
correct [kə'rekt] — richtig
couple of, a ~ [ə 'kʌpl əv] — ein paar
current ['kʌrənt] — augenblicklich, gegenwärtig
customer ['kʌstəmə] — Kunde/Kundin
customer care ['kʌstəmə keə] — Kundendienst
customer service [,kʌstəmə 'sɜ:vɪs] — Kundendienst
to **cut off** [,kʌt 'ɒf] — unterbrechen

D

dash [dæʃ] — Binde-, Gedankenstrich
date [deɪt] — Datum, Verabredung
deadline ['dedlaɪn] — Termin, Frist
to **deal with** ['di:l wɪð] — umgehen mit
definitely ['defɪnətli] — auf jeden Fall
delivery address [dɪ,lɪvəri ə'dres] — Lieferadresse
department [dɪ'pɑ:tmənt] — Abteilung
depends, that ~ [ðət dɪ'pendz] — das kommt darauf an
diary ['daɪəri] — Terminkalender
digit ['dɪdʒɪt] — (einstellige) Zahl, Ziffer
discount ['dɪskaʊnt] — Rabatt
to **discuss** [dɪ'skʌs] — besprechen, diskutieren (über)
disruption [dɪs'rʌpʃn] — Unterbrechung, Störung
distraction [dɪ'strækʃn] — Ablenkung
to **disturb** [dɪ'stɜ:b] — stören
to **double-check** [,dʌbl'tʃek] — genau überprüfen
doubt [daʊt] — Zweifel
to **drop** [drɒp] — fallen

E

echoing ['ekəʊɪŋ] — hier: Wiederholen
effectively [ɪ'fektɪvli] — effektiv, wirkungsvoll
efficiently [ɪ'fɪʃntli] — effizient, wirksam
engaged [ɪn'geɪdʒd] — besetzt
entirely [ɪn'taɪəli] — ganz, vollständig
equipment [ɪ'kwɪpmənt] — Geräte
exception [ɪk'sepʃn] — Ausnahme
excerpt ['eksɜ:pt] — Auszug
excuse [ɪk'skju:s] — Entschuldigung
existing [ɪg'zɪstɪŋ] — vorhanden
to **expect** [ɪk'spekt] — erwarten

expensive [ɪkˈspensɪv]	teuer
experience [ɪkˈspɪəriəns]	Erlebnis
explanation [ˌekspləˈneɪʃn]	Erklärung
extension [ɪkˈstenʃn]	Anschluss, Apparat

F G

face to face [ˌfeɪs tə ˈfeɪs]	persönlich, von Angesicht zu Angesicht
factory [ˈfæktəri]	Fabrik
family name [ˈfæməli neɪm]	Nachname, Familienname
fast [fɑːst]	schnell
fault [fɔːlt]	Fehler, Schuld
feasible [ˈfiːzəbl]	machbar
feedback [ˈfiːdbæk]	Rückmeldung
to figure sth out [ˌfɪɡər ˈaʊt]	etwas herausfinden
file [faɪl]	Datei
to fire away [ˌfaɪər əˈweɪ]	loslegen
to fix [fɪks]	regeln, erledigen
to forget [fəˈɡet]	vergessen
frustration [frʌˈstreɪʃn]	Enttäuschung
to get back to sb [ˌɡet ˈbæk]	jmd zurückrufen
to get through [ˌɡet ˈθruː]	durchkommen (am Telefon)
gradually [ˈɡrædʒuəli]	allmählich

H

hang on a moment [hæŋ ˌɒn ə ˈməʊmənt]	warten Sie einen Moment
to hang up [ˌhæŋ ˈʌp]	auflegen
to happen [ˈhæpən]	passieren, geschehen
hedge [hedʒ]	Einschränkung, Absicherung
to highlight [ˈhaɪlaɪt]	hervorheben, markieren
to hire [ˈhaɪə]	ein-, anstellen
to hold (on) [ˈhəʊld]	warten, am Apparat bleiben
honest [ˈɒnɪst]	ehrlich
to hurry [ˈhʌri]	sich beeilen
hyphen [ˈhaɪfn]	Bindestrich

I J

I'm afraid [aɪm əˈfreɪd]	leider
I'm sorry [aɪm ˈsɒri]	es tut mir Leid
ill [ɪl]	krank
immediately [ɪˈmiːdiətli]	sofort, umgehend
impolite [ˌɪmpəˈlaɪt]	unhöflich
to improve [ɪmˈpruːv]	verbessern
inconvenient [ˌɪnkənˈviːniənt]	unbequem, unpassend
ink cartridge [ɪŋk ˈkɑːtrɪdʒ]	Tintenpatrone
to install [ɪnˈstɔːl]	installieren, einsetzen
instructions [ɪnˈstrʌkʃnz]	Bedienungsanleitung
insurance [ɪnˈʃʊərəns]	Versicherung
internal [ɪnˈtɜːnl]	intern
to interrupt [ˌɪntəˈrʌpt]	unterbrechen
invention [ɪnˈvenʃn]	Erfindung
investment [ɪnˈvestmənt]	Investition
invoice [ˈɪnvɔɪs]	Rechnung
to involve [ɪnˈvɒlv]	einschließen, beinhalten
just in case [dʒʌst ɪn ˈkeɪs]	nur für den Fall

L

landline [ˈlændlaɪn]	Festnetz(leitung)
latest [ˈleɪtɪst]	letzte/r/s
latest, at the ~ [ət ðə ˈleɪtɪst]	spätestens
to let sb know [let ˈnəʊ]	jdm etwas mitteilen
line, on another ~ [ɒn əˈnʌðə laɪn]	auf einer anderen Leitung
line, bad ~ [bæd ˈlaɪn]	schlechte Verbindung

M

to make sure [ˌmeɪk ˈʃʊə]	sicherstellen
to manage [ˈmænɪdʒ]	(es) schaffen
market research [ˌmɑːkɪt rɪˈsɜːtʃ]	Marktforschung
marketing [ˈmɑːkɪtɪŋ]	Vertrieb
meaning [ˈmiːnɪŋ]	Bedeutung
to mention [ˈmenʃn]	erwähnen, nennen
message, to leave a ~ [liːv ə ˈmesɪdʒ]	eine Nachricht hinterlassen
message, to take a ~ [teɪk ə ˈmesɪdʒ]	eine Nachricht aufnehmen
mistake, by ~ [baɪ mɪˈsteɪk]	aus Versehen, irrtümlich
mix-up [ˈmɪks ʌp]	Missverständnis
mobile (phone) [ˌməʊbaɪl ˈfəʊn]	Mobiltelefon, Handy

to move [muːv]	weitergehen
to move forward [ˌmuːv ˈfɔːwəd]	vorangehen

N

necessary, if ~ [ɪf ˈnesəsəri]	falls nötig
to negotiate [nɪˈɡəʊʃieɪt]	verhandeln
network [ˈnetwɜːk]	Netz(werk), Sendenetz
nightmare [ˈnaɪtmeə]	Albtraum
noise, beeping ~ [ˌbiːpɪŋ ˈnɔɪz]	Pfeifton
noise, to make a ~ [meɪk ə ˈnɔɪz]	Geräusch/Lärm machen
note, to make a ~ [ˌmeɪk ə ˈnəʊt]	(sich) notieren, Notizen machen

O

office hours [ˈɒfɪs aʊəz]	Bürozeit
office space [ˈɒfɪs speɪs]	Bürofläche
operative [ˈɒpərətɪv]	hier: Mitarbeiter/in (im Call-Center)
opinion [əˈpɪniən]	Meinung, Ansicht
order, to place an ~ [ˌpleɪs ən ˈɔːdə]	einen Auftrag erteilen
out of stock [aʊt əv ˈstɒk]	vergriffen, nicht am Lager
over budget [ˌəʊvə ˈbʌdʒɪt]	den Finanzplan überschritten

P

PA [ˌpiː ˈeɪ]	(persönliche/r) Assistent/in
packaging [ˈpækɪdʒɪŋ]	Verpackung
to pay attention [peɪ əˈtenʃn]	achten auf
payment, means of ~ [miːnz əv ˈpeɪmənt]	Zahlungsmittel
to pencil sb in [ˌpensl ˈɪn]	jdn (vorläufig) vormerken
personal assistant [ˌpɜːsənl əˈsɪstənt]	(persönliche/r) Assistent/in
phone, over the ~ [ˌəʊvə ðə ˈfəʊn]	am Telefon
phone, to switch off the ~ [ˌswɪtʃ ˈɒf fəʊn]	das Telefon ausschalten
phone call, to make a ~ [ˌmeɪk ə ˈfəʊn kɔːl]	telefonieren
phone call, to receive a ~ [rɪˌsiːv ə ˈfəʊn kɔːl]	ein Gespräch entgegennehmen
to pick up [ˌpɪk ˈʌp]	aufnehmen
pitch, lower ~ [ˌləʊə ˈpɪtʃ]	tiefere Stimmlage
place name [ˈpleɪs neɪm]	Ortsname
planner (AE) [ˈplænə]	Terminkalender
point, to get to the ~ [get tə ðə ˈpɔɪnt]	auf den Punkt kommen
pointless [ˈpɔɪntləs]	sinnlos
possible [ˈpɒsəbl]	möglich, denkbar
post code [ˈpəʊst kəʊd]	Postleitzahl
to postpone [pəˈspəʊn]	verschieben
prepared to, to be ~ [bi prɪˈpeəd tə]	bereit sein
pretty [ˈprɪti]	ziemlich
previous [ˈpriːviəs]	vorherig, früher
probably [ˈprɒbəbli]	wahrscheinlich
product [ˈprɒdʌkt]	Produkt, Erzeugnis
production [prəˈdʌkʃn]	Produktion, Herstellung
to pronounce [prəˈnaʊns]	aussprechen
proposal [prəˈpəʊzl]	Vorschlag
prospective [prəˈspektɪv]	potenziell, voraussichtlich
provisionally [prəˈvɪʒənəli]	provisorisch, vorläufig
purchasing [ˈpɜːtʃəsɪŋ]	Einkauf
to put sb through [ˌpʊt ˈθruː]	jdn durchstellen

Q R

quietly [ˈkwaɪətli]	leise
quotation [kwəʊˈteɪʃn]	Angebot, (Kosten-)Voranschlag
radio operator [ˌreɪdiəʊ ˈɒpəreɪtə]	Funker/in
to reach an agreement [riːtʃ ən əˈɡriːmənt]	zu einer Vereinbarung kommen
to reach sb on [ˈriːtʃ ɒn]	jdn erreichen unter
to read back [ˌriːd ˈbæk]	(noch einmal) vorlesen
to read out loud [ˌriːd aʊt ˈlaʊd]	laut vorlesen
to rearrange [ˌriːəˈreɪndʒ]	umstellen
reason [ˈriːzn]	Grund, Begründung
reasonable [ˈriːznəbl]	vernünftig
receipt [rɪˈsiːt]	Quittung, Beleg, Bon
to refer [rɪˈfɜː]	verweisen, sich beziehen (auf)

relationship [rɪ'leɪʃnʃɪp] — Beziehung, Verhältnis
relationship, close working ~ — enge Geschäftsbeziehung
  [ˌkləʊs 'wɜːkɪŋ rɪ'leɪʃnʃɪp]
relaxed [rɪ'lækst] — entspannt, locker
relay switch ['riːleɪ swɪtʃ] — Relaisschalter
to **rent out** [ˌrent 'aʊt] — vermieten
to **repeat** [rɪ'piːt] — wiederholen
to **report** [rɪ'pɔːt] — berichten
to **respond** [rɪ'spɒnd] — reagieren (auf), antworten
response [rɪ'spɒns] — Reaktion, Antwort
responsibility [rɪˌspɒnsə'bɪləti] — Verantwortung
to **revise** [rɪ'vaɪz] — revidieren
to **rewrite** [ˌriː'raɪt] — umschreiben
right away [ˌraɪt ə'weɪ] — sofort, umgehend
to **ring back** [ˌrɪŋ 'bæk] — zurückrufen
to **rush** [rʌʃ] — hetzen, sich beeilen

S

saline solution [ˌseɪlaɪn sə'luːʃn] — Salzlösung
schedule ['ʃedjuːl] — Zeitplan
to **schedule** ['ʃedjuːl] — planen
to **screen calls** [skriːn 'kɔːlz] — Anrufe (heraus)filtern
self-conscious [ˌself 'kɒnʃəs] — hier: befangen
semiconductor [ˌsemikən'dʌktə] — Halbleiter
sent off, to get ~ [ˌget sent 'ɒf] — abgeschickt werden
serial number ['sɪəriəl nʌmbə] — Seriennummer
seriously ['sɪəriəsli] — ernst(haft)
set-up ['setʌp] — Aufbau
to **shift** [ʃɪft] — verschieben
shift work ['ʃɪft wɜːk] — Schichtarbeit
to **ship** [ʃɪp] — (ver)senden
similarly ['sɪmələli] — ähnlich
skill [skɪl] — Fertigkeit, Fähigkeit
to **solve** [sɒlv] — lösen
to **sort sth out** ['sɔːt aʊt] — in Ordnung bringen
to **speak up** [ˌspiːk 'ʌp] — laut(er) sprechen
to **spell** [spel] — buchstabieren
spontaneously [spɒn'teɪniəsli] — spontan
spreadsheet ['spredʃiːt] — (Tabellen-)Kalkulation
statement ['steɪtmənt] — Aussage, Feststellung
status report ['steɪtəs rɪpɔːt] — Statusbericht
step by step [ˌstep baɪ 'step] — Schritt für Schritt
straight away [ˌstreɪt ə'weɪ] — sofort, umgehend
subject, to change the ~ — das Thema wechseln
  [tʃeɪndʒ ðə 'sʌbdʒɪkt]

subsidiary [səb'sɪdiəri] — Tochter(gesellschaft)
successfully [sək'sesfəli] — erfolgreich
suddenly ['sʌdnli] — plötzlich
to **suggest** [sə'dʒest] — vorschlagen
suggestion [sə'dʒestʃən] — Vorschlag
to **suit best** [suːt 'best] — am besten passen
suitable ['suːtəbl] — passend, angemessen
to **summarize** ['sʌməraɪz] — zusammenfassen
supplier [sə'plaɪə] — Anbieter/in, Lieferant/in

T

tag, to play ~ [pleɪ tæg] — Fangen spielen
to **talk business** [tɔːk 'bɪznəs] — Geschäftliches besprechen
task [tɑːsk] — Aufgabe
technical support — (technische) Hilfe
  [ˌteknɪkl sə'pɔːt]
tentatively ['tentətɪvli] — vorsichtig, zögernd
tight [taɪt] — eng
time pressure ['taɪm preʃə] — Zeitdruck
time, at a ~ [ət ə 'taɪm] — hier: auf einmal
tone, after the ~ [ˌɑːftə ðə 'təʊn] — nach dem (Signal-)Ton
total ['təʊtl] — (End-)Summe, Gesamtbetrag
touch, to get in ~ [ˌget ɪn 'tʌtʃ] — sich melden
trade fair ['treɪd feə] — Handelsmesse
traffic, stuck in ~ — im Stau stecken
  [ˌstʌk ɪn 'træfɪk]
transceiver [træn'siːvə] — Sende- und Empfangsgerät
to **translate** [træns'leɪt] — übersetzen
to **type** [taɪp] — tippen

U V

unavailable [ˌʌnə'veɪləbl] — hier: nicht zu sprechen
uncomfortable [ʌn'kʌmftəbl] — unbequem
unit ['juːnɪt] — Stück
unit price ['juːnɪt praɪs] — hier: Stückpreis
urgently ['ɜːdʒəntli] — dringend
useful ['juːsfl] — nützlich
voicemail ['vɔɪsmeɪl] — Mailbox

W

welcome, you're ~ [jɔː 'welkəm] — bitte (schön)
whether ['weðə] — ob
white lie [ˌwaɪt 'laɪ] — Notlüge
to **worry** ['wʌri] — sich Sorgen machen
worst [wɜːst] — schlimmste/r/s
wrong number, to have the ~ — falsch verbunden sein
  [ˌhəv ðə rɒŋ 'nʌmbə]

Useful phrases and vocabulary

Opening a call

Identifying yourself
This is Leo Pearson from Griffin Plc.
It's Steve Zimmerman (from) AFS here.

Explaining the reason for the call
I'm calling about …
I have a question about …
I wanted to ask about …
Are you the right person to ask?

Getting through to the right person

Asking for the person
Could I speak to Bob Little, please?
Is Katja there, please?
Could you put me through to your accounts department, please?
Listen, Steve, I'm actually trying to get through to Paula. Is she there at the moment?

When the person isn't available
Oh, that's a pity. I'll try calling later.
Can I leave a message for him/her?
Can you ask him/her to call me back, please?

Taking a call

Identifying yourself
Micah Information Systems. Sylvia speaking.
HCE Ltd. Arno Maier speaking. How can I help you?
So, what can I do for you?

Transferring a call
Can I just ask what it's about?
Can you hold on a moment, please?
Can you hold the line, please?
I'll put you through.
I'm connecting you now.
The line's (still) busy.
Would you like to wait, or shall I ask him/her to call you back?
I'm afraid his/her line is engaged (AE: busy). Shall I give you his/her extension number?

When the other person isn't available
I'm afraid Ms Thoms is unavailable at the moment.
She's on another line/in a meeting/on a business trip.
I'm sorry, but Derek isn't in the office today.
Can I take a message?
Would you like to leave a message for her/him?
Would you like to call back later?
Can I help at all?

Calling someone back

Sorry, I'm really busy at the moment. Can I call you back later today/in ten minutes?
I'm actually talking to someone on the other line.
I think I've got your number, but can you give it to me again just in case?

Returing a call

I'm just returning your call from yesterday.
You left a message on my answering machine.

Ending a call

Thank you very much.
    → You're welcome.
Just let me know if there's anything else I can do for you.
    → I'll do that.
Speak to you later.
Bye now./Goodbye.

Communication problems

I didn't catch that (last part).
Could you repeat that, please?
Can you speak up a bit, please?
Could you speak a little bit more slowly, please?
Could you spell that for me, please?
This is a really bad line.
Sorry, we got cut off. … Anyway, as I was saying, …

Messages (in person)

Taking a message
Can I take a message?
Does (s)he have your number?
I'll tell him/her you called.
Shall I ask him/her to call you back?
I'll make sure he/she gets your message.

Checking the message
Let me just read that back to you.
Let me just make sure that I got that right.
You'd like to know if …
Was that M for Michael or N for Nancy?
Sorry, did you say 42 04 or 42 14?
Sorry, what was the post code again?

Leaving a message
Could you ask him/her to call me back?
My name is John Ellis. I'm calling from Retex Plc and my number is …

Messages (answering machines)

Greetings
You've reached Leze Logistics.
Unfortunately no one is available to take your call at the moment.
Our normal office hours are 9 to 5, Mondays to Fridays.
Please leave a message after the beep or send us a fax on (AE: at) ...
Hello. This is Cecilia's voicemail. I'm out of the office until 3 pm/the 5th. If it's urgent, please contact Jeff on (AE: at) extension 439. Thanks.

Leaving a message
This is Walter Jackson calling for Heike Lorenz.
I'm calling about ...
Maybe you can get back to me.
I think you have my number already, but here it is again just in case. It's ...
I'll be in the office until 6 pm today if you want to call me.
Hope to speak to you soon.

Mobile phones

Where are you?
→ I'm on the train.
→ I'm actually in the office. You can call me on my landline if you like.
→ I'm afraid I'm in a meeting at the moment. Can I call you later?
Have you got a couple of minutes?
My battery's low – we might get cut off, I'm afraid.
Sorry, you're breaking up (a little).
Listen, I think I'm losing the connection. I'd better go.

Small talk

Asking how someone is
How are you?
How are you doing?
How's business?
How are things in Frankfurt?

Answers
Fine, thanks. And you?
Not (so) bad.
A bit busy, as always.
Oh, can't complain. How are things with you?

Small talk questions
What have you been up to?
→ Nothing much, apart from work, to be honest.
→ I've just got back from holiday.
How's the weather over there?
→ Wet, as usual!
→ Really nice, for a change.
How was your holiday?
→ Very nice. We had a great time.
→ Don't ask! It was a complete disaster.

Making arrangements

Suggesting a meeting
Do you have time to meet next week?
I was wondering if you might have time to meet next week.
It would give us the chance to talk about ...

Suggesting times and places
When would suit you?
Where would you like to meet?
Would Monday be OK for you?
How about Wednesday morning?
Shall we say 10 o'clock in my office?
Maybe you can pencil me in on Tuesday morning.

Reacting to suggestions
I just need to check my diary.
I think that should be possible.
Tuesday's bad for me, I'm afraid.
I'm tied up all day.
Yes, that would be good for me.

Confirming an arrangement
OK, so I'll see you Wednesday, then.
So that's Monday at 10 am at your office.

Changing arrangements
I'm calling about our meeting tomorrow.
I'm afraid something has come up.
One of my clients has cancelled/brought forward our appointment.
The meeting lasted longer than I expected.
I wanted to ask you if we could meet a bit earlier/ postpone our meeting.
I was wondering if we could reschedule our appointment.
Would it be possible to meet a bit later?

When you are late for an appointment
I'm afraid my meeting has taken longer than I expected.
I might be a few minutes late.
I should be there by 3 at the latest.

Complaints

Making a complaint
Are you the right person to talk to?
There appears to be a small problem with your latest consignment.
There appears to be a mistake on the invoice you sent us.
You seem to have forgotten the attachment.
Some of the components don't seem to work.

Clarifying the problem
What's the problem exactly?
Could you explain the problem in more detail?

Apologizing
I'm very/extremely sorry about that.
Please accept my apologies.
That's entirely our fault.
There must have been a mix-up.

Taking action
It's good that you've brought this problem to my
    attention.
This is what I'll do.
I'll make sure it gets sorted out straight away.
Let me put you through to our accounts department.
    They'll sort it out for you.
You actually need to speak to our technical support
    hotline. Unfortunately I can't put you through
    directly, but let me give you the number.

Ending on a positive note
Again, I'm really sorry about the mix-up.
Well, thanks for sorting that out.
    ' It's the least I can do.
I'll personally make sure it doesn't happen again.
If you have any questions just give me a call.

Reaching agreements

Making proposals
I wanted to make a suggestion.
I have an idea.
What do you think?
How does that sound?

Interrupting
Sorry, can I interrupt you there?
Yes, yes, but can I just say something?
Well yes, that may be true, but...
Can I just come in here?
Can I just stop you there?

Reacting to proposals
That sounds feasible/very reasonable.
We could probably work with that.
That depends./That's difficult to say.
I don't think that would be possible.
I think we have a certain amount of room to
    manoeuvre, but I would have to check with my
    boss first.

Useful verbs (in content)

to call sb back	Can I call you back later today?	jdn zurückrufen
to catch	Sorry, I didn't catch your name.	verstehen
to connect	I'm connecting you now.	verbinden
to get cut off	Sorry, we got cut off. Where were we?	unterbrochen werden
to get back to sb on sth	I'm not entirely sure. Can I get back to you on that?	jdn wegen etw zurückrufen
to get in touch	I'm trying to get in touch with Mr Ellis.	sich melden, erreichen
to get through	I'm trying to get through to the sales department.	durchkommen
to hold	Could you please hold? I'll try to connect you.	warten, am Apparat bleiben
to leave a message	Would you like to leave a message for him?	eine Nachricht hinterlassen
to put sb through	Shall I put you through to Mr Seide?	jdn durchstellen
to reach sb on	You can reach him on his mobile.	jdn erreichen unter
to read sth back to sb	Let me just read that back to you.	(noch einmal) vorlesen
to receive a phone call	I received a phone call from your colleague yesterday.	ein Gespräch entgegen-nehmen
to return sb's call	I'm just returning your call from earlier.	zurückrufen
to spell	Could you spell that for me please?	buchstabieren
to speak up	Sorry, I can't hear you. Can you speak up a bit, please?	laut(er) sprechen
to take a message	I'm afraid he's in a meeting. Can I take a message?	eine Nachricht aufnehmen

British English / American English

British English	American English
(also) answerphone	answering machine
diary	planner
half (past) two	half past two
mobile (phone)	cell (phone)
on extension 439	at extension 439
send us a fax on 897 543	send us a fax at 543 2111
the line is engaged	the line is busy

Numbers, dates, times, symbols

Numbers

325	three hundred and twenty-five
6,148	six thousand, one hundred and forty-eight*
8,723,935	eight million, seven hundred and twenty-three thousand, nine hundred and thirty-five
3.1415	three point one four one five*
€45.89	forty-five euros, (and) eighty-nine (cents)
$23.53	twenty-three dollars, (and) fifty-three (cents)
0044 17 33 897 702	zero** zero four four***, one seven, three three, eight nine seven, seven zero two

*   A comma (,) in English shows thousands, and a
    point (.) shows the decimal place.
** British people often say 'oh' instead of 'zero'
    when saying telephone numbers.
*** In telephone numbers, 44 can also be said
    'double four' (BE).

Dates

The date 21 June 2005 can be said in different ways:
'the twenty-first of June, two thousand and five'
'June twenty-first, two thousand and five'
'June twenty-one, two thousand and five' (AE)

Remember that the date 01.02.06 means 1 February
2006 in Great Britain, but 2 January 2006 in the USA.

Times

The 12-hour clock is normally used on the telephone
So the time 14.00 is '2 pm', or '2 o'clock in the
afternoon' or just '2 o'clock' (often it is clear from the
context whether you mean am or pm). 14 o'clock and
2 o'clock pm are not possible in English.

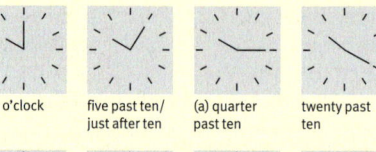

ten o'clock	five past ten/ just after ten	(a) quarter past ten	twenty past ten	half (past) ten

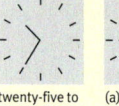   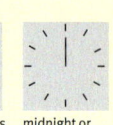

twenty-five to eleven	(a) quarter to eleven	ten to eleven	twelve minutes to eleven	midnight or noon/midday

Symbols

_	underscore	:	colon
@	at	;	semi-colon
-	hyphen	/	(forward) slash
–	dash	\	back slash
.	point (numbers), full stop/period (at the end of a sentence), dot (in an email or website address)	#	hash/pound (chiefly AE)/number
		*	asterisk/star
		(	open bracket
		)	close bracket
?	question mark	()	round brackets
!	exclamation mark	[]	square brackets